T0265903

What Readers Are Saying About
I Want to Trust You, but I Don't

"Lysa's words about trust came at a time when I desperately needed them. They gave me encouragement to open my heart up to the right people and to explore where my trust in the Lord was lacking and could grow."

—COLLEEN C.

"Just when you think Lysa can't be more vulnerable, she surprises you. This book caused me to think, to feel, and to be empowered with practical tools on how to trust when I feel my trust has been broken."

—HEATHER S.

"This book is a must-read for anyone who has experienced conflict, hurt, or trauma. Readers will find a treasure, a trusted friend, and a life-changing resource within the words beautifully crafted by Lysa."

—TESCIA J.

"Whether or not your trust has ever been broken, you need to read this book."

—LIZZY H.

"This book is for the girl who finds herself tangled in the tension of broken trust and fractured relationships. Lysa's honesty and vulnerability provide a safe space for me to heal from past hurts. This book has been the best resource to help me restore a responsible and wise level of trust in my relationships. I am confident it will be a blessing to anyone who reads it."

—MICHELLE M.

"Lysa writes in a way that makes you feel understood, like someone is finally offering the language you needed to describe what you are going through. She found her way back to trust, connection, and true relationships, and this book is just the guide I needed to do the same."

—GRACE F.

"In this book, Lysa discusses the topic of trust and gives practical ideas on how to deal with trust issues. She is honest, raw, real, and transparent in ways that will make you laugh, cry, and identify with how she has tackled trust issues in her own life. You will see God's Word and wisdom woven through this book. She does an amazing job walking you through a topic in a down-to-earth way, always pointing the reader back to God."

—LAUREN D.

"Broken trust in relationships has sadly become a culturally acceptable practice. You don't have to look far to find a friendship, marriage, or even a coworker relationship struggling to survive a betrayal of some kind. As any loving friend would do, Lysa gently encourages us to look betrayal in the face with hope. With a heart for her friends intent on healing wounds and bringing glory to God, Lysa provides a shoulder to cry on, an arm to lean on, and a compass to point us toward a better way. Lysa's guidance and practical tools provided in the pages of this book helped me to open my heart to rebuilding trust in God, in myself, and in my people. Thank you, Lysa."

—REGINA B.

"I am not sure I have words that can do justice for how amazing this book is. I cried, laughed, and had quite a few epiphany moments!"

—SHALOMIE L.

"Sometimes there are times in our lives when we have faced such hard circumstances that we feel completely isolated with our feelings and can't imagine that someone else understands the deep hurt we are navigating. Lysa not only understands it but does a remarkable job at putting words around those feelings that have left us speechless. I felt seen and understood and am thankful for her vulnerability and commitment to the truth at all costs."

—JESSICA C.

"Lysa's writing is a wonderful balance between anointed and practical. I found myself not only highlighting page after page but pausing and allowing myself to process. Lysa helped unravel the deep pain I was holding, not only against people but God. Thankfully, through the scriptures shared in this book and Lysa's revelation, I was able to get up and dust myself off. My trust in God has been restored, and for that I am eternally grateful."

—MADELYNN R.

Some Other Books and Video Bible Studies by Lysa

You're Going to Make It (devotional)
Good Boundaries and Goodbyes
Good Boundaries and Goodbyes Bible Study Guide and Video
Forgiving What You Can't Forget
Forgiving What You Can't Forget Bible Study Guide and Video
Seeing Beautiful Again (devotional)
It's Not Supposed to Be This Way
It's Not Supposed to Be This Way Bible Study Guide and Video
Embraced (devotional)
Uninvited
Uninvited Bible Study Guide and Video
30 Days with Jesus
40 Days Through the Bible
I'll Start Again Monday

Children's

It Will Be Okay
Win or Lose, I Love You!

I WANT TO TRUST YOU,

but I don't

*Moving Forward When You're Skeptical of Others,
Afraid of What God Will Allow,
and Doubtful of Your Own Discernment*

LYSA TERKEURST

NELSON
BOOKS

An Imprint of Thomas Nelson

I Want to Trust You, but I Don't

Published in Nashville, Tennessee, by Nelson Books, an imprint of Thomas Nelson. Nelson Books and Thomas Nelson are registered trademarks of HarperCollins Christian Publishing, Inc.

Thomas Nelson titles may be purchased in bulk for educational, business, fundraising, or sales promotional use. For information, please email SpecialMarkets@ThomasNelson.com.

Unless otherwise noted, Scripture quotations are taken from The Holy Bible, New International Version®, NIV®. Copyright © 1973, 1978, 1984, 2011 by Biblica, Inc.® Used by permission of Zondervan. All rights reserved worldwide. www.Zondervan.com. The "NIV" and "New International Version" are trademarks registered in the United States Patent and Trademark Office by Biblica, Inc.®

Scripture quotations marked CSB are taken from the Christian Standard Bible®. Copyright © 2017 by Holman Bible Publishers. Used by permission. Christian Standard Bible® and CSB®, are federally registered trademarks of Holman Bible Publishers.

Scripture quotations marked ESV are taken from the ESV® Bible (The Holy Bible, English Standard Version®). Copyright © 2001 by Crossway, a publishing ministry of Good News Publishers. Used by permission. All rights reserved.

Scripture quotations marked NASB are taken from the New American Standard Bible® (NASB). Copyright © 1960, 1962, 1963, 1968, 1971, 1972, 1973, 1975, 1977, 1995 by The Lockman Foundation. Used by permission. www.lockman.org

Scripture quotations marked NKJV are taken from the New King James Version®. Copyright © 1982 by Thomas Nelson. Used by permission. All rights reserved.

ISBN 978-1-4002-1183-8 (ePub)
ISBN 978-1-4002-5120-9 (IE)
ISBN 978-1-4002-5294-7 (CU)
ISBN 978-1-4041-2005-1 (CU)
ISBN 978-1-4002-5166-7 (CU)

Library of Congress Cataloging-in-Publication Data

Names: TerKeurst, Lysa, author.
Title: I want to trust you, but I don't : moving forward when you're skeptical of others, afraid of what God will allow, and doubtful of your own discernment / Lysa TerKeurst.
Description: Nashville, Tennesse : Nelson Books, [2024] | Summary: "New York Times bestselling author Lysa TerKeurst shows you what to do with your skepticism and distrust so you can heal from past betrayals and move forward with strength and resilience"-- Provided by publisher.
Identifiers: LCCN 2024012409 (print) | LCCN 2024012410 (ebook) | ISBN 9781400211821 (hardcover) | ISBN 9781400211845 (audiobook) | ISBN 9781400211852 (tp)
Subjects: LCSH: Trust--Religious aspects--Christianity. | Skepticism.
Classification: LCC BV4597.53.T78 T47 2024 (print) | LCC BV4597.53.T78 (ebook) | DDC 248.4--dc23/eng/20240516
LC record available at https://lccn.loc.gov/2024012409
LC ebook record available at https://lccn.loc.gov/2024012410

Printed in the United States of America

24 25 26 27 28 LBC 5 4 3 2 1

To Chaz: you helped me see that trust is possible. I love you.

Contents

•

CONTENTS

Broken trust complicates every bit of the

parts of love that should be comforting.

Introduction

Fear Has the Louder Voice Right Now

•

I want to trust you, but I don't.

I want to believe you have my best interests in mind, just like I do for you. I want to believe you don't have a hidden agenda, motivations that are completely self-serving, or something going on behind the scenes I would be crushed by if I knew about it.

I want to believe the good feelings I have when you are being kind to me will still feel good a month from now. A year from now. I want to believe you've told me the whole story and that I won't make discoveries later that make me cry and feel the brutal weight of regret. I want to believe I won't lie in bed sobbing over the red flags I missed or chose not to pay attention to.

I want to believe you aren't writing a narrative about me and our relationship that doesn't line up with the facts. I want to believe you have the ability to know right from wrong. I want to believe you are wise. I want to believe I can count on you. I want to believe you won't hurt me. I want to believe you won't talk behind my back. I want to believe that you are honest, good, fair, godly, kind, and accountable to do the right things and think the right things.

I want to believe your love is real and your care is genuine.

I want to believe my relationship with you will be calm and not chaotic.

I want to believe I'll feel wise and not stupid for trusting you.

I want to believe I'll forever love to tell the story of how we met and how long we've been this close.

I want to believe I'm safe with you and that you really are my person.

I want to believe I'll be okay if I trust you.

But I'm scared.

I've been burned before. So many times before.

I fear getting this wrong.

I'm unsure.

My anxiety tells me to run. But do I build my life around anxiety?

Are these trust issues really triggers from past pain? Or are these trust issues legitimate warning signs?

I want to be okay. I want us to be okay.

But I'm afraid the risks are just too high.

My heart says I love you, but my fear says it's not safe.

And fear has the louder voice right now.

So, I want to trust you, but I don't.

And this is where I put my head down on my desk. I don't know whether to cry or to hold this angst in and stare at the wall.

I want my closest relationships to have the assurance of safety, honesty, and stability. But we don't always get what we want. We get what we get.

Is this just my experience, or is this yours too? This is the confusion that first got me thinking I needed to do some work around my busted-up trust. If you've followed my journey, I don't need to catch you up on all the events that made me feel foolish for giving people access to the most vulnerable parts of my heart. But if you haven't, let me encapsulate it for you.

Friendship breakups. Loved ones not having my back. Several

deeply hurtful and life-altering betrayals. Lies. Gaslighting. Me feeling crazy. Me making shocking discoveries over and over. The death of my marriage. Another couple of friendship fractures. Time spent grieving. Being thankful some lost relationships could be repaired and restored. More grieving over other relationships that won't ever be the same. Wrestling with who I can trust and who I can't. Swinging the pendulum from being too trusting to being skeptical of just about everyone.

It was exhausting. But I wanted to move forward. Get on with my life. The problem was, being alone in the quietness of my house had become so much more appealing than opening my door, walking on, and trying to figure out how to trust again when mostly everyone felt unsafe. An annoying warning kept going off in my mind, like a smoke detector when the battery is low. It wasn't a full-on alarm, but the shrill chirp was not something I could just ignore either. Even as I forced myself to appear okay in front of others, the dialogue inside my head kept sounding the alarm: *Things aren't normal. People aren't good. You're risking too much trusting those who you think love you. Just when you think you are safe enough to open up a bit, they'll hurt you. They all have secrets. They all will eventually let you down, betray you. None of them can be trusted.*

Those thoughts turned into skepticism and eventually turned into an off-kilter belief system. Filtering everyone through my hurt was turning me into someone I'd never been before I was so deeply affected by having my trust broken. I felt suspicious about the real intentions of others. I started mentally filling in blanks in relational uncertainties with increasing suspicion.

Have you ever found yourself imagining all the *real* reasons your friend seemed distant the last time you saw them? Or tried to figure out the hidden agenda of family members who say one thing but you are certain mean something different? Or started making assumptions about a coworker after getting a weird feeling from them, mentally accusing them of what they're doing that could potentially put your job in jeopardy? Or questioned how much freedom you, as the boss, have given to an employee who is just giving you the bare minimum and can't possibly be working all the hours you are paying them for?

Sometimes, what we are sensing is spot-on and helps us know what needs to be addressed. But other times we are unnecessarily projecting things onto others that just aren't there. We don't want to get it wrong, but we also don't know what to do from here. These kinds of mental gymnastics are exhausting and make us hold back the very best of who we are for fear of getting hurt. That's exactly what was happening with me.

But it wasn't just other people causing my issues with trust to be at an all-time high. I was also questioning myself.

I was usually the one who believed the best about everyone and thought they had my best intentions at heart. It used to be easy to trust people. And in the few situations when I felt scared or not as sure of that trust, I calmed myself down by noting my own keen discernment. I was confident I would be able to detect if something were going sideways.

But then, after years of correctly sizing up situations, when I started getting hit with my own shocking discoveries, I was stunned by how much I'd missed—how many times I had given people the benefit of the doubt when I shouldn't have. What happened to my ability to sense when something was wrong?

Now I wasn't sure I could trust my discernment, which I'd always viewed as such a sweet gift from God. And I even started doubting I could fully trust God. I stopped having the passion I'd once had to read my Bible, go to church, or listen to worship music. I secretly questioned how a good God could see what was going on behind my back and not do anything to either stop it or help me find out before it got as bad as it did.

I don't want to admit this, but I felt betrayed by God. He had allowed so many things I didn't understand. In my mind, so much hurt could have been avoided if only He had intervened in ways that I assumed a good God would. And most confusing of all, my suffering felt never-ending while the people who hurt me continued to make choices that didn't honor God, yet seemed to be carrying on just fine.

All my skepticism and doubt about the people in my life, about my own discernment, and about God was turning me into someone I didn't even recognize. Someone I didn't want to be. I didn't want to give up on all relationships, but I also didn't know how to keep trying, knowing I may get hurt again. Trust just felt like a fool's game with way too much risk.

But life kind of requires us to be trusting.

When my daughter had her son, a wise nurse told us, "Trust is the oxygen of all human relationships." A relationship without trust is a relationship without vulnerability and depth. A relationship without trust is void of the kind of love we were meant to give and receive. A relationship without trust is one with very little vibrancy and eventually no life at all.

I'm not just talking about romantic love. I'm talking about all relationships where we want a deep connection that is both safe and lasting. When I feel that kind of warmth with a close friend or loved one, that's home to me. It's a haven that makes me think of what heaven will one day be like.

Remember in Genesis 2:25, "Adam and his wife were both naked, and they felt no shame." The lack of shame referred to in this verse means they were sinless and unbroken. They saw each other in their naked form and fully accepted the gift of each other with no fear. But on this side of eternity, sin has caused that kind of innocence and purity to be tainted. So what do we do?

What happens to a girl who feels forced to trust when she just simply can't? And what happens to a Bible teacher others expect to be unwavering but who feels overwhelmed with confusion about God, others, and herself?

The process of wading through all of this can feel like trying to run through quicksand. When I was in the middle of it, I couldn't just stop; otherwise I would sink and drown in all that hurt. But every step I tried to take to keep going forward took unusual effort, with a heaviness I couldn't get off me. I wanted to get through all of this quickly, but the pain made me hyperaware of every move. I felt forced to be in slow motion while everyone else was zipping past me at normal speed.

The shock of broken trust makes life feel painfully slow and uncomfortably fast at the same time. The disbelief that this is your reality makes everything grind to a halt. But the reality of jobs and bills and kids who need a ride to school all feels unrealistically normal, and normal feels too fast for a brain that can't process what's happening.

I want to fully acknowledge how difficult all of this has been on your heart and mine. I want to leave space for raw emotion that can so easily come to the surface when talking about events you may be still processing. But, mostly, I want to gently pass along something I've learned that I want you to hang on to as we keep turning these pages.

The trauma of having your trust broken by people you thought would never betray you is life altering. But it doesn't have to be life ruining.

That's why I wrote this book. I have walked the road of hurting and healing for years. There has been lots of counseling. Lots of internal work. Lots of praying and seeking. Lots of perspective shifts and healing. New hope. New discoveries. And finding a life that's so different from what I thought my future would look like. But finally realizing different can be wildly beautiful.

Now I'm walking forward in ways I never thought possible. And you can too. I want to hold your hand as we explore what's happened to us and how it affected not only our emotions but also our brains and central nervous systems.

The trauma of having your trust broken by people you thought would never betray you is *life altering*. But it doesn't have to be *life ruining*.

Yes, the damage of emotional hurt really does go much further than we think. And if you have people in your life who have minimized your pain or who don't understand how serious betrayals and broken trust really are, I want you to know, it's not that you're being too dramatic or overly emotional as you process all of this. The damage is real. I'm not just talking in theory here. I've seen what relationship dysfunction and trauma can do.

As crazy as this might sound, I had my brain scanned.

I went through a battery of tests and then several scans, because I wanted to know the facts. More than just feeling the impact of what I've walked through, I wanted to see it. I wanted to stare at the results with a doctor who studies this. And I wanted him to tell me what he saw and what story my brain scan was telling him. I wanted the truth.

Once I had my scans done, I sat down with Dr. Daniel Amen, a physician and psychiatrist specializing in brain health. Together, we compared my brain scans with the scans of a perfectly healthy brain. It was really telling to both of us that, as a result of experiences I've had, I now show clear evidence of what's called "the trauma diamond."

Dr. Amen has done studies of trauma survivors and found their SPECT (single-photon emission computed tomography) brain "scans show significantly increased activity in the limbic, or emotional, areas in a pattern that looks like a diamond."[1] As I sat there with him, looking at evidence of how all I've experienced in my life has impacted me, I felt, for the first time, I could use the words *emotional abuse* without flinching.

Here's the reality of how the affected areas of my brain have changed the way I process life and relationships:

- "Anterior cingulate gyrus: This region is the brain's gear shifter and helps you go from one thought to another. Too much activity here is associated with a fixation on negative thoughts or behaviors.

- Basal ganglia and amygdala: These are the brain's anxiety and fear centers, and overactivity is linked to heightened anxiousness and predicting the worst.
- Thalamus: The thalamus acts as a sort of relay station for the brain, and increased activity in this region heightens sensory awareness.
- In some people, the right lateral temporal lobe is also overactive. This area of the brain is involved in reading the intentions of other people. When activity here is excessive, people can misread cues from others."[2]

So the shift in how we process life situations and relationships after trauma is more than just our emotional reactions; it's a change that happens physically in our brains. The more I learn about the physical side of what happens to us when we are betrayed, the more it makes sense to me that so many of us have issues with trust. And that's not a bad thing we should be ashamed of. Nor is it a label we should put on ourselves—"Well, you know, I have trust issues"—like it's a disease or a diagnosis we can't ever heal from.

As a matter of fact, that day Dr. Amen showed me that the work I've done and continue to do is actually helping to heal my brain.[3] The counseling, Bible study, EMDR (eye movement desensitization and reprocessing; a type of mental health therapy to help "alleviate the distress associated with traumatic memories"[4]), and taking better care of my brain through supplements and a healthier lifestyle is working. I remember my counselor once saying to me, "We have more hope and help than you have problems." I now see that he was right. And I want to share that hope and help with you. So, I pray this book will be a significant and important part of your healing process.

Having trust issues makes so much more sense when we have some of these facts.

I also want to bring to light that the anxiety often accompanying our fears around trust may be trying to serve us, not hinder us. Though we want to keep it in check and not let our anxiety spiral out of control, we should also know God designed our bodies to detect when situations or people are not safe. Think about the natural instinct of an animal when it senses danger. Though we are different from animals, Job 12:7–13 tells us that God designed us with the same creative brilliance to use our senses and discernment to pick up on danger.

The increased anxiety we experience when we are unsure about trusting others doesn't mean we are broken. But we do need to learn how to bring these feelings back to a healthy level so we can have better discernment and more clarity.

You've got questions about this, and I do too.

Can I rebuild trust with the person who hurt me? Or is distrust the wisest choice here?
Can I discern if someone is really being honest?
Can I still trust God?

These are good questions that deserve to be explored. I can't promise you that I'll have all the answers you need. But I've learned so much that I wanted to invite you into my journey, to share the transferable wisdom I've gained, the tools that have been helpful, the setbacks, the victories, and the deepest wrestling I've ever done with questions about myself, others, and even God.

The subtitle of this book is exactly what I feel passionate about for both of us: *Moving Forward When You're Skeptical of Others, Afraid of What God Will Allow, and Doubtful of Your Own Discernment.*

I understand the fear of trying again. I know the heartbreak of having to let go of some relationships with people I shouldn't trust. I know the hesitancy in trying to repair some relationships to see if trust can be given again. And I know the resistance to meet new people and explore if, how, and when you can trust them.

But I also know the joy of moving into new seasons. I know the thrill of feeling safe enough to connect deeply with people who are trustworthy. I know how much courage it will take to keep walking into a future full of possibilities.

And I promise you the risks are worth taking.

Now, let's go learn a thing or two about trust.

One More Thing I Want You to Know

Okay, so usually this section after each chapter is to give you a little deeper research or insight into that chapter. But since this is the introduction and I'm feeling a little protective over you, I have something I want you to know in case this has ever happened to you: no one has any business labeling others with "trust issues" when we *all* have them.

I have to get this off my chest, because when someone says another person has "trust issues" like it's a bad smell that person puts off, I believe they are announcing their own lack of awareness and compassion. If I'm honest, one of the reasons I didn't want to admit I had trust issues was because that term has been used against me.

Here's the truth: if someone is struggling to trust, chances are there's a reason. Whether they can recall the exact reason or not, they've had an experience that has made them recoil in angst and pain. Of course they are hesitant or possibly resistant to trusting people, especially those who have hurt them or who remind them of someone they trusted and got burned by. It makes sense that they are skeptical of other people's intentions. And of course they analyze people with a heightened awareness of the irresponsible and cruel ways humans sometimes act.

Sometimes distrust is the most appropriate response there is.

I think that's been true of a lot of the distrust in my life that makes me uncomfortable, hesitant, and sometimes resistant to engage with certain people. My issue with trusting those people may honestly be a sign of wisdom, not weakness. And my tendency to overanalyze their words and actions, or even a feeling I get when I'm around them, may actually be an exercise of discernment, not deficiency.

Other times, I have trust issues that are more of an indication of past traumas I still need to work on than of the person in front of me doing anything deceitful. Or I have trust issues because I don't want to risk people getting close enough to hurt me like I've been hurt before. There are many reasons we can find ourselves grappling with trust, reasons that are sometimes good and sometimes not so good.

Here's a crucial thing to remember: not one of us gets to live this life unmarked by hurt. So not one of us gets to live this life without trust issues. Maybe that makes you feel comforted. Maybe that makes you feel unnerved. This will be a tension to manage, not a problem to solve. As humans, we are made for connection. But connection always comes with risk. But having the right tools to better navigate this is what so many of us have been missing in order to move forward. Feeling understood in our hurt and learning how to use these tools in a safe atmosphere of hope and healing is where we are headed in these pages. It's good to know we are in this together.

As humans, we are
made for *connection*.

But connection

always comes

with *risk*.

Remember (Statements to Cling To):

o The trauma of having your trust broken by people you thought would never betray you is life altering. But it doesn't have to be life ruining.

o God designed our bodies to detect when situations or people are not safe.

o Sometimes distrust is the most appropriate response there is.

o As humans, we are made for connection. But connection always comes with risk.

Receive (Scriptures to Soak In):

"The LORD will guide you always;
      he will satisfy your needs in a sun-scorched land
      and will strengthen your frame.
You will be like a well-watered garden,
      like a spring whose waters never fail." (Isaiah 58:11)

"Does not the ear test words
      as the tongue tastes food?
Is not wisdom found among the aged?
      Does not long life bring understanding?"
         (Job 12:11–12)

Reflect (Questions to Think Through):

o When you think of the word *trust*, what are some situations, good or bad, that instantly come to mind?

○ How have you experienced having your trust broken by people you thought would never betray you? What impact has this had on your life?

Pray:

Heavenly Father,

Thank You for leading me here. I ask for Your help, guidance, and wisdom. As I move forward and process the ways I've had my trust broken, I know You are with me to help me walk this road toward healing. Thank You for being right beside me and for being a trustworthy Father.

In Jesus' name, amen.

Chapter One

Quietly Quitting on Hope

•

If you and I were sitting together talking today, just us, it wouldn't be long before I'd want the conversation to go beyond the initial awkwardness of pleasantries and dive into the deep places. And the topic I'd want to get to is the way we sometimes quietly quit on hope. I bet we both have reasons for wanting to quit, especially when we've hoped for something for so long that now it's starting to make us feel foolish. It's brutal to hope for this thing that, in your mind, makes so much sense. So why isn't our good God making it happen?

Your soul can feel a bit rubbed raw from opening yourself up to the possibility of "it" happening. You grip tightly onto the confirmations that seem to point in the direction of your prayers being answered. Like in a game of tug-of-war, you give it your all to hang on. Then, the resistance finally seems to lessen, the rope starts getting pulled in the right direction toward you, and you smile so big, knowing the moment is finally close . . . but then suddenly the rope is yanked by the opposition and you fall flat on your face. Your blistered hands and your exhausted soul sting as the hope you were clinging

1

to is ripped away. The tighter you were holding on, the worse it hurts when it's pulled away.

To manage the disappointment, you may say things like:

"It's just better if I reduce my desire for this down to a zero."

"Maybe it's not meant to be, and I'm good with that."

"I'm actually okay being alone, because I just don't have it in me to make a new friend."

"I just don't care about this any longer."

"I must not be built for this."

"I made some really foolish decisions in the past, so I don't deserve what I've been praying for."

But then you cringe inside, because you know you're saying something with your mouth that your heart desperately disagrees with. But what choice do you have? You have cried out to God more times than you can count, yet nothing seems to be coming through. His silence is deafening. The results are shocking. The betrayal is crushing. The outcome is so disappointing. The way you were treated is maddening. The tears you cry in the darkness of night seem never-ending. Another "no" is disillusioning.

You really believed this friendship would be lifelong.

You really believed you would be healed.

You really believed he would come back.

You really believed you'd get pregnant.

You really believed your parents would eventually be proud of you.

You really believed your child would be okay.

You really believed you would meet the man of your dreams.

You really believed this company had your best interests in mind.

You really believed this leader cared about you and this was a
safe place to plant deep roots.

You really believed God's answer would line up with what you
prayed for.

So, quitting on hope seems like the only reasonable choice to
make at this point. After all, hope is the most brutal risk of all.

I get it.

For me, hope is either the most beautiful feeling of possibility or
the worst feeling of defeat. To dare to hope is to simultaneously expose
our greatest desires and our greatest fears. But if we're not willing to
risk hoping, then we are already quietly quitting on a better future.
The hardships of today will feel so much heavier when we limit our
view of life to the hardships of right now. We will trade dreaming for
dread. We will exchange looking forward with joy for looking back-
ward with sorrow. We will swap the anticipation of future possibilities
for the angst of staying stuck in the pain of what happened.

When we quit on hope, we will become blind to the evidence of
God's goodness all around us. And if we lose sight of God's goodness,
trusting Him will feel foolish. It's difficult to keep trusting God and
other people when we feel they constantly let us down and don't come
through for us.

Sometimes we need new perspectives to start to believe trust is
possible. That God is still good. And that there are still good people
out there. But that's really hard to hear when your life doesn't look
like you thought it would and relationships aren't playing out like you
hoped.

You've received enough hurt and bad news. It's high time to now
receive some hope. Instead of filling our thoughts today with all the
worst-case scenarios we fear, I want to challenge us to stop and say,
But what if it does *all work out?* Now pause and let that new question have some space in your thoughts. I can make the choice to stop

To dare to hope is to simultaneously expose our greatest *desires* and our greatest *fears*.

feeding the anxiety and instead start fueling hope by recounting the many everyday moments where God *has* come through for me and where things *did* work out. For example, "I made it to work safely this morning," "That bill did get paid," "My child passed that test," "My body was healthy enough to do all that I did today," and so on. Just because these are small things that didn't hit my radar doesn't mean they are insignificant things. They are all evidence that more times than not, things really do work out okay, and that fuels my hope for today. Again, this isn't denying there are still hard things happening, but remembering all that *is* working out will help bring balance to our thoughts. I find great comfort in the truth of Ecclesiastes 7:14: "When times are good, be happy; but when times are bad, consider this: God has made the one as well as the other. Therefore, no one can discover anything about their future."

While we may not know the exact details of the future, we can trust and hope in a good God who does (Romans 15:13). When we start to feel hopeful again, we can start believing our future still contains good possibilities. Believing there is good ahead of you will give you the courage to try to trust again. And I want to make sure, as you dip your toes into this journey back to healthy trust, that you are equipped with the right tools to help this process not feel so daunting, scary, and impossible.

Having the right tools is crucial. And that's why we'll spend the rest of this book learning to use new tools I'll share with you. But it's not just about having tools; it's also about having the confidence to use them.

I saw this play out a few years ago when I was getting ready to speak at a church conference. I was sitting backstage, feeling the usual pre-message jitters, when the event coordinator asked if I would wear an oblong plastic device hooked to my shirt. Thinking this was a modern version of a lapel microphone, I explained that I was just using a handheld mic, so there was no need for a clip-on.

An anxious look crossed her face. She went on to explain there was a woman in the audience who had asked if I would wear this as a special favor so she could better hear my message. I wanted to do this for the audience member, no question. But not really understanding the situation, I grew concerned. I didn't want my blouse to droop in places that would make me hyperconscious, and there didn't seem to be any inconspicuous way to wear the new device. Trust me, I've been in many embarrassing situations while standing onstage, and I try to avoid adding any more stories like these to my life.

Thinking of other possible solutions, I went to find the sound guy. I asked him if I could clip the device onto the podium or my Bible as long as I stayed close enough for it to still properly work. That's when I was given more explanation. For forty-five years, the lady in the audience had never been able to hear a sermon being preached. She'd actually never even heard a prayer being prayed. Her doctor had been working on this special device that would send the specially magnified sound of my voice directly into her hearing aids, allowing her to listen as never before. Me wearing this clip wasn't just a special favor. This was an epic event in this woman's life.

Now that I'd heard the whole story, I felt like such a heel for worrying about my shirt. I clipped the device directly below my chin and suddenly couldn't have cared less about the shirt droop. I walked onstage and immediately asked my new friend if she could hear me. With blinking eyes and a huge smile, she nodded. Several times during my message, she had tears streaming down her face. So did her friend who was with her. By the time I concluded with a prayer, I knew this was an incredible victory for her lifelong struggle.

It's amazing what a gift it is to be able to hear. I guarantee you, of all the hundreds of people in the audience that day, there was no one listening with more intentionality than my friend with the device. She knew she needed help to hear. The device filled a gap she couldn't fill on her own. Once she made use of it, she was able to listen . . . really listen.[5]

Most of us don't have the same hearing challenges this sweet woman has. But the way trust has been broken or eroded in some important relationships has been painful and confusing, and it has diminished our hope down to the faintest of whispers. Honestly, at times, hope is completely blocked all together. I want the voice of hope to break through, and I want this book to be the device that helps us hear it loud and clear.

Why is it important to reignite our hope as we seek to work on trust issues? Because without hope that things can get better, we'll just stay stuck. We'll let the pain of what has happened to us negatively impact us to the point where we no longer want to open up our hearts and be fully alive in other relationships. We aren't made to live in fear of getting hurt and hesitant for connection. We aren't made to let skepticism be our primary filter through which we see God and others. We aren't made to constantly doubt ourselves and feel we can't even trust our own discernment.

We aren't made to let skepticism be our primary filter through which we see God and others.

We were made to love and to be loved. We were made to embrace others. We were made to be wise and discerning. We were made to live with assurance of God's faithfulness. We were made to hope and rise back up with resilience. We were made to be fully alive. So, let's go figure out what to do with our busted-up trust.

One More Thing I Want You to Know

Throughout this book, I want us to use compassionate processing. Sometimes you'll come across some sentences or paragraphs that feel too much for the most tender parts of your heart. Other times, you may be tempted to personalize and turn the information against yourself, wishing you had chosen more wisely with certain relationships. Or something will require you to be honest about things that for years you have pretended are better than they are. All of this has been true of me walking through this message for myself.

I had to learn to be gentle with myself. That doesn't mean I don't acknowledge things I need to do better or develop in, but it does mean I won't beat myself up for things that happened in the past. We can't change what happened then, but we can change what happens from here on out. As we learn, grow, and gain new insights, we will be gentle with where we still feel fragile and at the same time be brave with taking steps forward.

Here's a list of compassionate statements we can say out loud to ourselves and revisit when necessary.

* I'm going to be honest with myself and stay committed to reality throughout this process. I won't sugarcoat or make things look better than they are.
* I will not take responsibility for or try to fix other people. I will own only what is mine to own.
* I will be compassionate toward myself, realizing that when you know better, you do better. The fact that I picked up this book shows I want to know better so that I can do better.

❋ Instead of shaming myself for not picking up on the red flags in previous relationships sooner, I'm going to choose to feel appropriately convicted to make better choices in the future. I'm not going to believe the lie that it's too late to change.

❋ I will acknowledge I'm a victim of hurt, but I'm not going to live as a victim. I am now going to be empowered to take charge of my own healing.

❋ I still believe there's a beautiful world with wonderful people to connect with, to laugh with, to dance with, to explore with, to live with, and to have purpose and make a difference with.

❋ I am now willing to learn how to trust my own discernment again, how to appropriately trust the right people, and how to trust God even when I don't understand what He's doing.

This kind of compassionate processing has given me the freedom to acknowledge what I can work on without beating myself up for trust mistakes I've made in the past. And it's also given me the courage to see myself as someone who will rise up and keep going.

Remember:

○ To dare to hope is to simultaneously open up to our greatest desires and our greatest fears.

○ When we quit on hope, we will become blind to the evidence of God's goodness all around us.

○ Hope is the most brutal risk of all.

○ We aren't made to let skepticism be our primary filter through which we see God and others.

9

Receive:

"When times are good, be happy;
      but when times are bad, consider this:
God has made the one
      as well as the other.
Therefore, no one can discover
      anything about their future."
      (Ecclesiastes 7:14)

"May the God of hope fill you with all joy and peace as you trust in him, so that you may overflow with hope by the power of the Holy Spirit." (Romans 15:13)

Reflect:

- What are some of the statements you commonly say to yourself and others to help manage your disappointment? *(See the list at the beginning of the chapter.)*
- What life circumstances have tempted you to want to quit on being hopeful?
- Which one of the compassionate statements in the "One More Thing I Want You to Know" section resonates with you the most and why?

Pray:

Lord,

I want to keep hope at the forefront of my mind in the days ahead. Help me give myself grace and accept Your grace as I learn and grow in this area of trust in my relationships. I'm feeling fragile, yet brave, in this process. Steady me and continue to speak life into my weary soul as I work through this message and apply it to my life.

In Jesus' name, amen.

Chapter Two

What Is This Feeling . . . Discernment or a Trigger?

.

2015

The goodbye seemed rushed. Seeing a suitcase being wheeled away from me set off alarm bells. There was an awkwardness I didn't understand. My pulse quickened, and I could feel my throat tighten. I tried really hard to blink away the tears. I told myself over and over, *I trust him. I trust him. I trust him. I trust him.* But then why was my mind at war with this trust? My thoughts were a tangled mess, trying to figure out what was really going on.

The possibilities coursing through my mind felt like daggers to my heart. *You are not safe. There's something going on you don't know about. And if you did know about it, it would crush your heart. Don't you dare trust him. It's not worth the risk.*

But then my mind shifted to a different internal dialogue.

You are safe. You're reading into this situation more than you should.

And if you bring up your concerns, you're going to stir up unnecessary conflict. You'll seem like the crazy one here. It's not worth the risk.

And then another shift in my thinking.

Something is terribly wrong. My hands started shaking. *Do something. Say something!* But while my brain was racing, my words felt stuck somewhere down inside me. I could not form a sentence. I could not find my voice. I was screaming on the inside but silent on the outside.

And another shift.

Get it together, Lysa. This is ridiculous. There's nothing wrong. Remember all the kind words he said yesterday? Manage these feelings so you don't make a big deal out of this and stir up drama.

Now, here's the sad part. In this instance, I absolutely should *not* have trusted. I was discerning that something was wrong, and I was right. There was absolutely something wrong going on.

2023

Several years later, long after my divorce, I faced a similar scene. This time, it was with someone I was dating. He hadn't given me any reasons to distrust him. He treated me well. He told the truth. He was where he said he would be. He didn't act suspiciously or like he was covering anything up. Yet that day, his goodbye seemed rushed. And because a rushed goodbye in the latter years of my marriage meant something was wrong, seeing a suitcase being wheeled away from me set off alarm bells.

It was as if I couldn't tell the difference between then and now. It didn't matter that this was a completely different person; the feelings were the same. It felt as if the past was repeating itself.

There was an awkwardness I didn't understand. My pulse quickened, and I could feel my throat tighten. I tried really hard to blink away the tears. I told myself over and over, *I trust him. I trust him. I trust him. I trust him.* But then why was my mind at war with this trust? My thoughts were a tangled mess as I tried to figure out what was really going on.

The possibilities coursing through my mind felt like daggers to my heart. *You are not safe. There's something going on you don't know about. And if you did know about it, it would crush your heart. Don't you dare trust him. It's not worth the risk.*

But then my mind shifted to a different internal dialogue.

You are safe. You're reading into this situation more than you should. And if you bring up your concerns, you're going to stir up unnecessary conflict. You'll seem like the crazy one here. It's not worth the risk.

And then another shift in my thinking.

Something is terribly wrong. My hands started shaking. *Do something. Say something!* But while my brain was racing, my words felt stuck somewhere down inside me. I could not form a sentence. I could not find my voice. I was screaming on the inside but silent on the outside.

And another shift.

Get it together, Lysa. This is ridiculous. There's nothing wrong. Remember all the kind words he said yesterday? Manage these feelings so you don't make a big deal out of this and stir up drama.

In this case, I absolutely *should* have trusted. I was discerning that something was wrong, but I was wrong. There was nothing going on that would hurt me.

In the first situation, what was firing in my mind was discernment. It was a warning I should have listened to. In this second situation, what was firing in my mind was a trigger from past trauma. Confusing, isn't it? The line between healthy discernment and triggers caused by pain from the past is paper-thin.

My discernment rarely comes with immediate details. It's a feeling prompted by the Holy Spirit.

And my triggers rarely come with immediate details. They are feelings prompted by pain from my past.

I have to pray through and sort through both.

Sometimes a trigger from a past situation provides experiential wisdom that ushers in discernment. Like I said, a paper-thin line.

Is this a warning that could protect me? Or is this a war in my mind I need to work through? How do I know if this is discernment? Or possibly fear? Or a trigger because of past trauma? I want to be wise so I can protect myself. But I also don't want to cause those around me who are trustworthy to unfairly suffer through my suspicions fed by past betrayals.

And that's the struggle with trust for me. I would imagine you have wrestled with this at times too.

In typical Lysa fashion, I couldn't just sit with these questions. I felt I had to have some kind of checklist or scientific research or something to help me know what to do when warning bells went off in my head. I read and researched and processed this with friends. One of those friends also happens to be a licensed professional counselor who understands on a very personal level the healing journey I'd been walking. She has had her own experience wrestling with trust as well.

She said my questions were good and understandable. My brain was trying to figure out if I was safe or not. The uncertainty was causing me to feel anxious. And given what I'd been through in the past, it's no wonder I felt so unsure.

But she encouraged me to set my questions aside for just a bit. Instead, she wanted me to tell her more about what I was experiencing in my body and what story I was telling myself because of those feelings.

When the goodbye felt rushed and I saw him load his suitcase into his truck, I immediately felt shaky. My emotions felt too big to swallow. Fear. Disappointment. Pain in my chest. The story I told myself was that there was a reason the goodbye was quick, and that reason would be very, very hurtful to me. And that there was information being withheld from me. When I eventually got the full story, it would shatter my heart all over again.

She nodded, again letting me know she understood and acknowledging that the way I was feeling was connected to the relational trauma I'd been through that ultimately had led to divorce. Then she said something profound: "That suitcase experience in this new relationship was too close to the edge." In other words, my nervous system was letting me know I was too close to a situation that had hurt me previously. And connecting these two experiences made my fear skyrocket. Rushed goodbyes in my previous relationship made this rushed goodbye feel like betrayal could be happening all over again.

Some people believe worst-case scenarios don't ever happen. My experiences beg me to believe otherwise. But automatically assigning the betrayal and deceptions from a past relationship to a brand-new relationship would not only be unfair and potentially damaging—it could be detrimental.

"So now what?" I asked. I felt stuck. I didn't want to bring this hard stuff up and potentially damage this new relationship. But I also couldn't pretend that I wasn't concerned.

Without hesitation, she replied, "Investigate."

Her confidence in telling me to investigate was jarring but also empowering. I had spent years in my previous relationship so afraid to investigate because I thought the only thing that would get proven in the end was that I had trust issues. That I was crazy. That I was letting my ever-increasing anxiety cloud my judgment. Plus, I wanted to believe the best about this person I loved.

To investigate felt so wrong to me.

But in hindsight, what was actually wrong was that I was once in a relationship where I felt the need to investigate but was too afraid to do so. So, instead of looking into things to verify what I was being told, I just kept asking questions, hoping to get answers that made sense. But things just weren't adding up. And when I pressed for more explanation, I was shamed for my concern. So, my central nervous system was doing the job God created it for. It was firing off constant warning signals. But then I felt incapable of figuring out what the warning was about.

Friend, please lean in close here.

It is okay to need more information.
It is okay to ask questions and verify what is true.
It is okay to be honest about what we can and cannot handle.

My counselor, Jim Cress, taught me the human brain is always in search of confidence in knowing. In other words, as much as is possible, I need to know what's going on so I can be confident that I'm safe.

But facts aren't the only things we need to pay attention to when assessing whether it is safe to trust another person. Feelings are also crucial. Safety is both fact and feeling. Therefore, trust is both fact and feeling. I don't just need to be told I'm safe; I need to believe it for myself. Otherwise, my neurological makeup will trigger the automatic defense strategies of fight, flight, or freeze. This process is called *neuroception*.

I don't just need to be told I'm safe; I need to believe it for myself.

Okay, this is about to get a little heady, but we are smart girls and this stuff is fascinating. Plus, think how fun it will be to casually bring this up with your friends over coffee like you have known this all your life. Your friends will be like, "Whoa . . . impressive!"

I found this fascinating research on neuroception, a concept originally developed by psychologist and neuroscientist Dr. Stephen Porges:

> Essentially, neuroception is the process by which neural circuits determine whether a situation or person is safe, dangerous, or life-threatening. As opposed to perception, which is a cognitive thought, neuroception involves brain processes that work outside of conscious awareness. Neuroceptive evaluations can occur extremely quickly and without your knowledge. If social cues trigger a neuroception of safety, our bodies enter a calm behavioral state. We feel calm and can easily engage with others socially or attend to issues. . . . When situations appear risky, the specific areas of the brain regulating defense strategies are activated. Then even neutral or social behavior is met with aggression or withdrawal instinctively.[6]

Well, that explains why I'm constantly trying to evaluate safety before connection. If someone feels unsafe to me, I withdraw. I've never understood why I feel such an intense sense of unsafety, even when a person isn't physically threatening me. When I feel emotionally unsafe because of something someone says or does, I have an immediate desire to also get away from that person or at least to give them as little information about my life as possible. So, for me, when I feel emotionally unsafe, I have a physical reaction.

I find it so interesting that, from the very beginning of time, we see this same physical reaction to fear and distrust play out with people in the Bible. (If you know me, you know I have an obsession with Genesis chapters 1 through 3 . . . so here you go!) In Genesis 3, when Adam and Eve ate the forbidden fruit and their eyes were opened not just to their nakedness but also to the knowledge of evil, they surely felt a sense of fear. How did they react when God came near them? They withdrew and hid. Then they got defensive and accusatory— Adam blaming the woman and the woman blaming the serpent.

This same pattern is found later in the Bible too. Let's not forget the reaction of the disciples when Jesus was arrested (you can read about it in Matthew 26:47–56, John 18, and the other Gospels). They withdrew. They denied knowing Him. Even Peter, who drew his sword and cut the ear off Malchus (a servant of Caiaphas, the high priest) in defense of Jesus, withdrew when his hopes of revolution failed and Jesus was taken into custody. He denied Jesus three times. What a swing of emotions—first being so confident that he drew his sword and then, the next moment, feeling fear settle in after an awareness of what, from an earthly perspective, seemed like Jesus' failure. Peter ran into hiding.

Hi. It's me. I have this reaction too. When situations feel risky, I want to withdraw. Every now and then, I'll get loud and say things more directly than I normally would. And sometimes I do both. It's not that these reactions are necessarily bad, unless they become unhealthy ways to cope. If my reactions start damaging the relationship, then it's a problem.

With the second of my two suitcase scenes, the issue wasn't that this person was engaging in secretive activities that would betray my trust. Nor was the issue that I'm too broken from the past to trust again. The real issue was that I didn't know a suitcase being wheeled away would be a problem. I didn't know it would impact me with such force. My body couldn't settle down and feel safe in the context of a rushed goodbye. So, I withdrew inside myself. And I just wanted to run away from the situation entirely.

I've since learned this is a pretty common response for those of us with hurts that cut us to the core. Every trauma has two parts to it: the fact of what happened and the impact it had on us. When we dismiss our feelings and what those feelings are trying to tell us, our initial instinct can be to numb, to ignore, to override, or to shame ourselves for having them. Let's get really personal here and see what each of these responses look like played out.

1. Numb

Sometimes it is hard for me to even figure out what I'm feeling when I get flooded with fear and anxiety. And when I can't immediately attach the feelings I'm having to the exact reason for them, it makes me feel on edge and hypersensitive. When the suitcase situation happened in my new relationship, I remember telling my friends, "I'm having big feelings" around a situation that would be small to other people. I had a choice to either feel the pain so I could get to the root cause or do something to just get the pain to go away.

Some people numb out by binge-watching TV. Others by drinking too much alcohol. Others operate in extremes. We overexercise, overwork, overeat, or become overbearing by taking control of other people or situations. Or we go to the opposite end of the spectrum and become lethargic, unmotivated, unable to eat, or withdrawn.

It's interesting that we take this route of numbing to deal with emotional pain, similar to how doctors sometimes numb our bodies to help us avoid physical pain. Social psychologist Dr. Naomi Eisenberger explained it this way:

> A lack of feeling connected with others creates pain—not only the discomfort of loneliness, but symptoms analogous to physical pain. In fact, some of the same brain regions that respond to physical pain also respond to "social pain"—the painful feelings associated with social rejection or loss.[7]

Who knew emotional pain and physical pain were so closely connected? But her research further revealed that "taking Tylenol actually reduced 'hurt feelings'—experiences of social isolation and rejection."[8]

Even a Tylenol bottle warns us that if the pain continues, we need to seek medical attention. We don't want to make this temporary pain relief a permanent solution that prevents the body from sending us a signal that something more needs to be examined. Pain drives us to be more urgent about addressing what needs to be addressed. If we numb our feelings, we will miss the warning they may be trying to send us. Or we'll be prevented from looking under the hood to explore what's going on internally.

2. Ignore

Another route we sometimes take in response to fear is to ignore our feelings. A recent *Time* magazine article shares some interesting information about the dangers of stuffing down our feelings:

> Emotions have energy that pushes up for expression, and to tamp them down, our minds and bodies use creative tactics—including muscular constriction and holding our breath. Symptoms like anxiety and depression, which are on the rise in the U.S., can stem from the way we deal with these underlying, automatic, hard-wired survival emotions, which are biological forces that should not be ignored. When the mind thwarts the flow of emotions because they are too overwhelming or too conflicting, it puts stress on the mind and the body, creating psychological distress and symptoms. Emotional stress, like that from blocked emotions, has not only been linked to mental ills, but also to physical problems like heart disease, intestinal problems, headaches, insomnia and autoimmune disorders.
>
> Most people are ruled by their emotions without any awareness that this is happening. But once you realize the power of emotions, simply acknowledging your own can help greatly.[9]

This is really convicting for me to read. Why is it that sometimes I would rather avoid being honest with my feelings so I don't have to deal with an unpredictable reaction from others? I think I stuff my feelings, hoping things will just get better on their own. Other times, I don't want to get vulnerable enough to risk people having access to my tender feelings. Then there are other times when I'm too busy or there seem to be more important things to deal with, so I just keep plowing through life, acting like I don't have the very real feelings that I'm stuffing.

The problem with all of this is that I will eventually pay the price for this kind of stuffing. Either the emotions will cause damage inside me or they will one day erupt like a beach ball that finally breaks free from being held underwater. Stuffing seems okay until I realize undealt-with emotions over time run a high risk of causing more damage than I ever thought. My counselor often reminds me, "What we don't work out, we act out."

3. Override

When I feel afraid, I sometimes jump to a statement of wisdom or a scripture to quickly get over the pain and force myself to just be okay. It is good and right to rely on wisdom and the power of the Holy Spirit, who always guides us to God's truth. But we shouldn't override the message our fears and angst may be trying to tell us.

Honest confession . . . I treat my emotions as if they are a sign of spiritual immaturity. I can catch myself pretending I'm not feeling the emotions that are happening inside me. Then I find myself weaponizing Scripture against my emotions instead of using truth to help me process them. For example, I will quickly quote a verse like 2 Timothy 1:7: "For the Spirit God gave us does not make us timid, but gives us power, love and self-discipline." God's truth isn't shaming me because I have fear but rather reminding me not to get consumed by it. It's okay to feel the fear and hear the message it may be trying to send me.

I WANT TO TRUST YOU, BUT I DON'T

God wants us to pour out our hearts to Him about whatever is troubling us. We see this modeled throughout the book of Psalms. There is so much angst and fear and turmoil expressed without the pressure to tidy it all up or minimize the hurtful realities. God isn't disappointed in our raw honesty with Him. The beautiful thing is that this is exactly what He wants from us. And then through our prayers and lament and vulnerable processing, He can guide our feelings and help us stay aligned with His truth.

4. Shame

Why aren't you stronger, Lysa? Can't you just get it together? Mind over matter! Get a grip! You shouldn't be so sensitive. You should be able to handle this. You shouldn't make such a big deal out of things. You should just get over this and move on. You shouldn't overreact like this.

Maybe some of the harsh statements you say to yourself sound a little bit different than mine. I asked some of my friends how this plays out for them, and they said things like: "You should be past this by now." "You just need to deal with this." "Don't be dramatic. Just brush it off." "Just keep saying you're fine so other people don't think you're weak." "Get it together—other people can handle this, so why can't you?"

But do you know the most dangerous part of what all this shaming can do to us is? It can make us short-circuit our need for healing just because we are embarrassed to be human. Humans sometimes break. We hurt when we break. It takes time and intentionality to heal our breaks.

Imagine someone saying the previous statements to you if your leg had a compound fracture. Would you tolerate their demands to stop being so sensitive or for you to get over it so others don't think you're weak? Absolutely not. Sometimes I shame myself with statements I wouldn't ever tolerate from other people. Healing requires tender care. I'm so very tender with others; I guess it's time I learn to give myself that same level of compassion. It's wise not to run with broken bones or rush through our broken hearts.

When we are triggered, anxiety and fear will naturally emerge. But instead of numbing, ignoring, overriding, or shaming ourselves, let's acknowledge there's a reason our body is activated and alarmed. Then we can take the time to let those feelings inform us to look into this situation further. That doesn't mean we let these feelings run rampant and turn into catastrophic thinking. But they shouldn't be ignored either.

I bet you have been told the exact opposite. I have. After all, Jeremiah 17:9 says, "The heart is deceitful above all things and beyond cure. Who can understand it?" Doesn't this mean we should dismiss our feelings so we aren't led astray by them? No. It means we shouldn't place our trust in our feelings and just "follow our own hearts" without God's truth guiding us, challenging us, and giving us the right path forward. Interestingly enough, Jeremiah 17 is entirely about the folly of misplaced trust.

But just because our feelings shouldn't dictate what we do doesn't mean we should ignore them completely. A warning light on your car dashboard doesn't tell you how to fix the issue at hand, but it serves a purpose in letting you know something needs to be looked into further . . . sooner rather than later. Just like physical pain is our body's way of informing us that something needs to be tended to, emotional pain operates the same way. If I feel afraid, it's my body's way of telling me to pause, think, consider, investigate, ask questions, and process what's really going on. If you don't feel safe with someone, you can't possibly trust them.

Feeling safe is a crucial part of the process of risk evaluation.

In order to trust, I must have the knowledge and the feeling that I am safe. So, ask yourself these questions:

- What is making me feel unsafe right now?
- How can I further investigate what my feelings might be trying to warn me about?
- Is there a reason I don't want to ask questions of the person causing me concern?
- Who can help me process this and help me decipher how serious this warning is?
- What do I need to hit the Pause button on until this is more settled?

Asking these questions doesn't mean we will get quick solutions to our concerns. But it will mean we are making the wise choice not to ignore them. Admitting we have concerns is a big step toward better understanding where our trust issues are coming from. So, back to our original question: "What is this feeling . . . discernment or a trigger from the past?"

I would propose to you, it's both. A trigger may mean more healing is needed. Discernment may be telling us to take it slow. Our past informs us of what can go wrong. Our present discernment reminds us to investigate. If both of these are done with the motivation of feeling safe, then there should be lots of grace for this desire, especially when we've been repeatedly hurt.

And if the other person we are in relationship with, whether it's a new relationship or one where we are trying to repair broken trust, has an issue with our need for ongoing healing, time, and safety, then that may be the most telling warning sign of all. Of course, none of this should be taken to an extreme, but it's okay to say you're not okay and then take the time you need to figure out why.

You're not a bad person or a crazy person for having uncertainties around trust. You're a person who takes relationships seriously and who wants to invest your heart deeply in the right ways with the right people. I'm proud of the bravery you and I have as we keep showing up, believing the right relationships will be worth it all.

One More Thing I Want You to Know

When trust has been broken in a relationship, trust issues can only be worked on in the context of relationship. That doesn't mean we must return to that previous relationship where we got hurt to work on trust. (If that's possible, then that's great. However, sometimes that may not be possible or safe.) But what it does mean is we can't isolate ourselves and work on repairing trust alone.

If trust was broken because of a relationship, trust has to be repaired through safe connection inside of a relationship. Trust requires both safety and connection.

Can I just tell you I really didn't like the information in that last paragraph one bit when I was fresh off of experiencing heartbreak and betrayal? I wasn't sure anyone was safe. All I wanted to do was withdraw from others. My heart was fragile. My nervous system had been working in overdrive for so long that the least little thing could trigger a flood of fear and emotions in me. I was having out-of-proportion reactions to situations I used to be able to handle with ease. The thought of trying to feel safe in another relationship was incomprehensible to me . . . especially another romantic relationship.

So I didn't start with working on trust in a relationship with another man. I wasn't ready, and that was okay. More than okay. I think it was wise. I started trying to feel safe in relationships where there had been consistent safety and trust for a long time. That may sound strange, but when my trust was shattered by my marriage that ended, I started feeling skeptical of everyone. I remember one day looking at my best friend, who I have trusted without hesitation for years, and wondering, *Do I really know her like I think I know her?* I was so frustrated with myself until I understood this makes sense. I never thought others would hurt me, but now I know even seemingly good people are capable of breaking my trust. I started with making notes of all the many ways she repeatedly proves she's trustworthy.

- She shows up when she says she'll be there for me.
- She tells the truth.
- There aren't weird inconsistencies in her stories.
- She holds private what I tell her in confidence.

So, in the safety of that relationship, as well as a few others, I started to see that trust was possible with the right people.

Then there were other relationships I still wanted to pursue, but I had to draw healthy boundaries around topics that were triggering for me. It's not that they were necessarily unsafe relationships, but giving those people too much information about my private world was not helping my journey toward repairing trust.

With each of my relationships, I had to be honest about what I could handle and what I could not during this season where trust felt risky and my heart felt fragile. But the point is, I couldn't hide away from people and work on trust.

It took me several years to branch out past people I already knew to even consider trying to trust new people. I knew the biggest test of all would be going on an actual date with a new guy. After putting clear boundaries and safety measures in place, I felt my heart was willing to at least try. We'll talk about the ups and downs of that more in another chapter, but the suitcase situation eventually happened with a safe man who was willing to lean in when I pulled back. Who was willing to unpack what I was feeling without personalizing it and getting defensive. Who was willing to come up with a plan so future goodbyes wouldn't be rushed or triggering. And who was willing to give me access to information about his activities and whereabouts. And you know what's really interesting? Because of the way he handled my concerns over the rushed goodbye, I didn't need any of that additional information he offered. The way he was patient and gentle with me gave me a wonderful feeling of safety. And from there I realized that, over time, trust could be possible.

But please hear me: *he* didn't fix my trust issues. That was an inside job I had to work on for several years before I ever met him. This is true with new friendships and even with repaired relationships with family, coworkers, and others I've known for a long time. While trust has to be repaired in the context of relationships, we can't expect others to be our source of mental and emotional stability. We have to gain that stability through healing what's been traumatized inside us. We must do the healing work inside us so we can do relational work with others around us.

So here's where I've landed with all this wrestling with trust:

I need to be gentle with myself.

I need to acknowledge what I'm feeling and what story I'm telling myself because of those feelings.

I need to ask questions. Like my counselor says, instead of getting furious, I need to get curious.

We must do the healing work *inside us* so we can do relational work with others *around us.*

Instead of making accusations, I need to do appropriate
investigation.

And the best thing the other person can do? They can be
gentle as well.

Together, we can acknowledge, "Of course this is happening. It's understandable. Let's just work together to get you the
answers you need."

Not everyone will be patient and willing to walk through
and talk through situations of trust concerns like this. But I'm
discovering the people I most likely should trust are willing.

Remember:

- The line between healthy discernment and triggers
  caused by pain from the past is paper-thin.
- We shouldn't place our trust in our feelings and just
  "follow our own hearts" without God's truth guiding us,
  challenging us, and giving us the right path forward.
- I don't just need to be told I'm safe; I need to believe it
  for myself.
- Pain drives us to be more urgent about addressing
  what needs to be addressed.
- We must do the healing work inside us so we can do
  relational work with others around us.

Receive:

"And do not be conformed to this world, but be transformed
by the renewing of your mind, so that you may prove what

the will of God is, that which is good and acceptable and perfect." (Romans 12:2 NASB)

> "For My thoughts are not your thoughts,
> Nor are your ways My ways," says the LORD.
> "For as the heavens are higher than the earth,
> So are My ways higher than your ways,
> And My thoughts than your thoughts." (Isaiah
> 55:8–9 NKJV)

Reflect:

- In what ways do you struggle to distinguish discernment from anxious thoughts about a situation?
- What do you think of when you read these statements?
  - » *It is okay to need more information.*
  - » *It is okay to ask questions and verify what is true.*
  - » *It is okay to be honest about what we can and cannot handle.*

Pray:

God,

This pain is deep, and this pain is real. Help me discern my next steps when I want to numb out, ignore, override, or shame myself in response to being activated and triggered by what's in front of me. Remind me of Your truth and Your plan for me when I just want to hide or despair. Give me the courage I need to ask good questions and put wisdom at the forefront of my thinking.

In Jesus' name, amen.

Chapter Three

Red Flags and the Roots of Distrust

•

My friend Linda asked if we could meet for coffee. She knew I was working on a book about problems in relationships, and she wanted help processing why a treasured friendship she'd had for years was suddenly a source of great angst. Linda and her friend (we'll call her "Christi") had been best friends for a couple of years. Their lives were intertwined. They shared meals, vacations, and family time. They laughed hard, prayed for each other, vented to each other, and counted on each other for support through good times and bad.

But there was one thing that drove Linda a little crazy. Christi was starting not to keep important promises she had made and forget events in Linda's life. She'd forgotten Linda's birthday and when Linda mentioned it, Christi had laughed and said, "We celebrate each other all the time anyway." Or she'd promise to watch Linda's kids but then act aloof about her commitment and not keep her word when Linda showed up. She wouldn't apologize and admit she forgot.

Instead, she made her other plans more of a priority, which left Linda in a real bind.

Linda was pretty easygoing, so she'd been understanding about these memory lapses.

Until lately.

She'd been feeling irritated and annoyed at Christi. And if she was honest, she felt hurt, like she wasn't important enough to be remembered.

Christi would not acknowledge her actions were inconsiderate and started making Linda feel like she was expecting too much from the friendship. At the same time, Christi fully expected Linda to show up for her whenever she got into a bind or wanted Linda's support.

Linda began to feel a disconnect, and she was growing more and more hesitant to keep engaging with Christi. When I told her she was dealing with roots of distrust, she was kind of shocked. She said, "It's not that I don't trust her; it's that I feel like I can't count on her." She wasn't making the connection that Christi's pattern of not showing up and keeping her promises was revealing the concerning characteristics of being inconsistent and insincere. As a result, trust was eroding in this relationship.

Before understanding this was all related to trust issues in their friendship, Linda saw the red flags of Christi forgetting and blowing her off but didn't know how to address them. She just kept thinking it was better to manage her feelings internally so she didn't get into a conflict with Christi without knowing how to verbalize exactly what was bothering her.

As Linda processed with me, I realized I could relate to this story on so many levels. And maybe you can too.

I've experienced this kind of confusing, mismatched affection, which, over time, can make you feel so used, foolish, and taken advantage of. What makes this even more complicated for me is that I keep thinking the other person will turn things around, since overall they've been a good friend. It's just that, over time, what at first felt like occasional mistakes have turned into a pattern of behavior, eating away at my confidence and trust in them.

I could tell you about so many relationships in my life where I didn't acknowledge the red flags until I started feeling like I could no longer trust the person. And here's the deal: if you let these red flags continue and the person keeps displaying these characteristics for longer and longer, the impact on you will multiply greater and greater. At first, a red flag could seem like a very small concern. But if it keeps happening and goes unaddressed, it can become a defining hardship that breaks the relationship.

When I hear "red flags," I think about the ones that are put up at the beach when there are conditions that shouldn't be ignored. A red flag is a warning that the riptide is too strong and you should not swim in the ocean. In other words, if you ignore this red flag, you are swimming at your own risk. If you jump in that ocean, completely ignoring the clearly posted red flag, you may suffer severe consequences.

Red flags aren't there to annoy you or be a killjoy on your beach day. Those red flags are there to protect you.

In the same way, red flags in our relationships alert us to issues we need to pay closer attention to and probably address. Red flags we ignore don't typically fix themselves—they just get to be more and more of an issue. Eventually, they can become serious breaches of trust. So, it's pretty important to be aware and acknowledge these red flags. They can be warnings that something is off with someone we are in a relationship with. Or at least a sign there are things that need to be discussed.

Most of the time, I will start to have a gut feeling of discernment that just keeps pricking at my thoughts but won't go away. I've always described discernment as a deep-down knowing. It's the ability to pick up cues that allow us to recognize subtle differences and inconsistencies, perceive when something isn't as it should be, and instinctively feel when someone is being dishonest.

Like I said before, the hardship of discernment is that it doesn't always give you details. But just because you don't know everything doesn't mean you shouldn't pay close attention to the red flags you do see. I like to think of discernment as the intimate way God cares for me, leads me, redirects me, warns me, and reveals things to me I otherwise may miss on my own.[10]

So many times, my brain and my heart come into conflict, especially when it comes to relationships I very much want to continue. My brain will fire off a warning, but then my heart will try to override it because I want to believe this person I love wouldn't deceive me . . . that they truly care about me. My heart will make excuses to try to quiet down the warnings my brain is sending.

Maybe your heart is more skeptical, and you find it difficult to trust anyone. Each time your discernment fires, it's just more confirmation to keep most relationships at arm's length because there are very few people you trust. People think you are incredibly thick-skinned, unaffected by the actions and words of others, and intimidating or standoffish. The truth is, you are incredibly tender inside. Your actions are the result of making a vow to yourself for self-protection so others can't even get close to wounding what feels so vulnerable inside you.

However you are wired, when your brain is sending the signal that something is off or unsafe, you need a way to wisely examine reality. Part of using wisdom with your discernment is to avoid extremes. As we just discovered in the last chapter, both safety and connection are important in a relationship. And neither should be taken to such an extreme that it excludes the other.

Hyperdesire for safety can mean low levels of connection.
Hyperdesire for connection can mean low levels of safety.

I'm not being wise if I constantly override my need for safety just to keep the connection with someone going. And the reverse is also true. If I take my need for safety to such an extreme that I want to avoid all the risks of a relationship, then I will have very little connection with others.

These two words, *safety* and *connection*, are directly linked to the health of the trust in a relationship. Maybe you aren't struggling with taking safety or connection to extremes, but you are in a relationship with someone who starts giving you fewer and fewer feelings of connection. Most likely you'll start to feel less and less safe, like the story of Christi and Linda. Or, like in the case of a wife finding alarming charges on her husband's credit card, that indication of a breach in financial safety can diminish her feelings of connection with him.

What we want is safe connections with others. That's why paying attention to red flags and knowing how to wisely discern what they may be telling you is important.

Even in good relationships, red flags may pop up from time to time. Maybe your feelings of alarm just need a clarifying conversation, and then you can determine this isn't a real red flag, just a misunderstanding. Or maybe the red flag is being caused by a

Safety and connection are directly linked to the health of the trust in a relationship.

small issue with a minor impact. We'll get to some ways to gauge how serious the red flags are a little later. But please know a red flag doesn't always mean the relationship is unhealthy or destined to fall apart. It may mean some work needs to be done and some intentional and honest conversations need to take place. Instead of letting these things fester in a relationship, the sooner we tend to what's diminishing our trust, the better. Feelings of trust can ebb and flow in relationships because we are all imperfect humans. There should always be a foundation of safety and connection with grace for occasional mishaps. But we shouldn't be afraid inside a relationship.

Some people believe when you love someone, you must give them

I WANT TO TRUST YOU, BUT I DON'T

unconditional trust. I understand the sentiment of this. And I wish all relationships were absolutely safe, honest, and in keeping with the way the Bible teaches us to treat one another. I wish there were absolutely no chance for either person to make decisions that break trust. But we all know that's not possible on this side of eternity. So instead of shooting for unconditional trust where we are blind to red flags and expected to overlook them, we need to shift from blind trust to wise trust.

If the thought of not giving unconditional trust makes you bristle, I get it. I used to think that too. But straight talk here: if I had continued to give unconditional trust in my previous marriage, that would have required me to overlook behaviors that were unacceptable and destructive to me. God may sometimes call you to leave room for Him to move in a relationship where there are red flags. I did this as well. But during that season it was necessary and wise to have clear boundaries and conditions to the trust in need of repair.

Wise trust requires us to take an honest look at reality. While people sometimes lie with their words, the truth eventually emerges in their actions. I remember once complaining to a trusted friend that I just couldn't tell what was true and what wasn't with someone who had broken my trust. She replied, "Really? Because this person's actions are speaking a message that's pretty clear to me."

And she was right.

There were red flags with the person I was struggling to trust. Those red flags were indicating characteristics that were very concerning. This person's actions were negatively impacting the safety and connection in our relationship. And the more information I got, the more I realized this person hadn't just diminished the trust between us; this person had absolutely broken it.

Like I just mentioned, red flags serve us best when we make good use of our discernment. So, let's dig into this a little more. Discernment is what gives us the ability to exercise insight "beyond the facts that were given."[11]

We need to shift from *blind* trust to *wise* trust.

Discernment is something we are called to as Christians. Jesus promised us before He ascended to heaven that He was leaving the Holy Spirit with us. And the Holy Spirit leads us into truth (John 16:13). In other words, the Holy Spirit who indwells us will equip and lead us to discern between the wisdom of God and the foolish ways of the world. We aren't to enable or excuse away behaviors that go against the wisdom of God. We are to be discerning.

We are to be discerning with our own behavior. But we are also to be discerning about our relationships. And the things God calls us to, He always equips us for. As Proverbs 17:24 says, discerning people make it a priority to keep the pursuit of wisdom always in front of them. One way we can pursue wisdom and practice discernment is by making the commitment to ourselves that we will acknowledge and appropriately address the red flags in our relationships.

In the following pages, we'll go through a list of concerning characteristics that may be underlying red flags you are seeing. This isn't something we want to use against another person in accusatory ways or to unnecessarily stir up issues. But it is a tool to help us find some much-needed clarity and discernment as well as some helpful language for having healthy, productive conversations. We can use this list to better understand the red flags we are sensing and where the roots of our distrust may be coming from. (Not all red flags are created equal. In the "One More Thing I Want You to Know" section, I'll give you a tool to help you gauge how serious some of these concerns might be.)

As you read through these red flags, you'll notice some seem very close in meaning. Don't get tripped up by the similarities of meanings and examples. Each red flag serves a purpose in helping us pick up on characteristics in others (and ourselves) that will bring clarity as to why we may be experiencing trust issues. As different relationships come to mind, remember to give yourself time to sit with and pray through some of the harder revelations. We want this information to help us discern the level of trust or distrust we have with the other person. It is meant to give us clarity on where the root of our trust issues may be coming from in relationships that are potentially problematic.

Red Flag #1: Incongruity

This person wants people to perceive them in one way, but then they act in a completely different way. Their words don't match how they actually live on a day-to-day basis. In other words their insides don't match their outsides.

Examples:

- They say they're hardworking but don't have a job and always have an excuse as to why it's someone else's fault. Then they expect others to provide for them so they can live the lifestyle they desire.
- They say they are taking seriously their doctor's advice to eat healthy, but their credit card statement reveals a lot of trips to fast-food restaurants.
- They present themselves as a spiritual giant who is wise and mature, but they lack restraint, don't treat people with kindness and patience, are selfish, expect to be treated as special, think they are superior to others, or believe the rules apply to others but not them.

Red Flag #2: Inconsistency

This person makes you feel on edge because you never know what version of them you will get on any given day. Sometimes they are kind, but sometimes they are not. Sometimes they act like they love you, but sometimes they seem cold and indifferent. Look, we all have bad days

I WANT TO TRUST YOU, BUT I DON'T

on occasion, but this is more of a pattern of duality that confuses you and makes the relationship feel unstable.

Examples:

- You aren't sure whether they would defend you or betray you if they heard someone say hurtful things about you.
- They assure you they won't share private information but then you find out they used it to prove a negative perception of you.
- They regularly offer to watch your kids while you and your spouse go out on a date but often cancel at the last minute when it becomes inconvenient or "too much."
- The stories they tell differ in truth and accuracy depending on the audience.
- Their behavior or mood changes drastically depending on their circumstance. They are easily enticed to act in unhealthy ways when things aren't going well for them.

Red Flag #3: Insincerity

An insincere person will tell you something they think you want to hear, but they don't actually mean it. You get an uneasy feeling when they compliment you or half-heartedly make plans with you. You often question whether they are sincere, because after being with them, you tilt your head and think to yourself, *Did they really mean that, or did they just put on a show to make themselves appear nice, caring, and interested?*

Examples:

- They say something nice just to end an argument because they cannot handle confrontation. Or they are buttering you up in an effort to appease you because they are secretly hiding something.

- They say they really care about you but call or text only when they need something from you.
- They tell you they want to meet up with you but are never willing to make definite plans.
- You feel exhausted after being with them because of all the mental gymnastics involved with trying to discern their true intentions.

Red Flag #4: Self-Centeredness

This person thinks only about themselves. It's as if the world revolves around them. They don't think about how their words and actions impact other people. They can be thoughtless and rude, but when you address this with them, they say things like "I'm just being honest" or they accuse you of being too sensitive. They believe they are always right. They want what they want and think their needs take precedence over others'.

Examples:

- In conversation, they keep the discussion focused on them and what they are going through. They rarely, if ever, check up on you and what you are facing.
- They are not bothered by making people wait on them. They do not consider other people's time as valuable as theirs.
- On the rare occasion you do try to pour your heart out to them, they brush you off, minimize your pain, and then try to one-up you by telling you why their struggle is way more serious than yours.

- They borrow your car, but when you get it back, there's no gas and they left trash inside.

Red Flag #5: Insecurity

This person lacks confidence in themselves so much that it creates a deep-rooted fear inside of them that you'll leave them. They expect you to say enough and assure them enough that it puts an exhausting burden on you to try to fix them. It's like they want you to convince them they have good qualities that they aren't even sure are true. This person can be jealous even though there isn't a legitimate reason. They need incessant encouragement to feel more stable in their relationships. They are excessively worried about your loyalty and commitment to them.

Examples:

- They tend to need you in unrealistic ways and are too dependent on you to help stabilize them or make them feel better about themselves.
- They get upset at you for talking with other people instead of them when you attend a party together, because they are unsure of themselves and their ability to branch out on their own.
- They are constantly asking, "Are we okay?" because they are unusually anxious about your relationship, even if there are no signs there is reason to worry.
- They get upset with you when you don't get on board with something they're doing and hold it over your head that you aren't showing enough support.
- They are easily offended because they believe everything has a deeper, negative meaning toward them. They are continually looking for reasons to prove you don't care for them.

Red Flag #6: Immaturity

This person acts childish. They don't think through the consequences of their choices. When they get caught, it's always someone else's fault. When something hurts them or they don't get their way, they have temper tantrums or pouting episodes.

Examples:

- They tend not to own the part they contributed to a conflict, saying, "But you . . ." in response.
- Their regular behavior tracks with someone much younger and less emotionally developed than their actual age and stage of life.
- They lack self-awareness and seem emotionally tone-deaf.
- They feel the consequences of their irresponsibility should suddenly become your emergency.

Red Flag #7: Immorality

This is someone who lacks a moral compass and disregards the principles of right and wrong. They see no problem with engaging in sinful, illegal, mean, insulting, or vile behavior. They may appear upstanding in some environments while actively participating in a secret double life.

Examples:

- They steal money from their parents' home when they visit because they feel they are entitled to what their parents own or have earned.
- They engage in extramarital affairs and addictive porn use—which is destructive to themselves, their spouse, and others around them—with no remorse or plans to stop.
- They easily justify lying and cheating to get ahead in their

profession. They see their behaviors as necessary to get what they desire and feel they need to stay on top.

- They compartmentalize secret parts of their life and don't feel convicted about lying, gaslighting, and doing whatever it takes to protect their sin.

Red Flag #8: Insubordination

This person rejects reasonable authority. If someone tries to hold them accountable, they retaliate against the one in authority and often start a smear campaign against them. They play the victim. They don't have a teachable spirit and lack the ability to see that guidelines exist for the greater good of the community.

Examples:

- They regularly drink and drive without any concern for what might happen to themselves or others if they do.
- They refuse to take their boss seriously when given a warning or are unwilling to receive reasonable correction or feedback at work or from another healthy leader in their life.
- They push against and refuse to honor the boundaries of other people.
- They are a leader who doesn't want to be held accountable by a board of directors, despite the fact they are living in violation of the very principles they teach others.

Red Flag #9: Incompetence

This person says they are capable of doing something you already know they don't have the training, experience, or track record to carry out. They won't acknowledge their inability until it becomes a problem too big to deny. They try to compensate for their lack of ability with convincing conversations about their progress, but behind the scenes things aren't happening like they should be.

Examples:

- They say they don't need to spend money on a plumber because they can replace the toilet just fine, but they actually don't know what they're doing.
- They volunteer to teach a seminar on a topic they are not well-versed in, and they have no expertise or experience doing what they are wanting to teach others. For example, they want to teach a class on managing finances when they are in major credit card debt.
- They promise to find someone to take care of an issue, but then, without researching reviews, they hire someone who does a terrible job.

Red Flag #10: Irresponsibility

This person is reckless. They tend to gravitate toward doing something fun over taking care of business. It's not that they are necessarily spiteful, but they don't take things as seriously as they should. They aren't a good judge for how much time something will take to accomplish. They are easily distracted from what's most important so they can enjoy whatever comes up in the moment.

Examples:

- They say they're going to pay an important bill on time, but then you get a final notice and realize they didn't take it seriously or follow through.

- They offer to run by the grocery store for you, but they didn't write everything down on your list and leave out a crucial ingredient you needed for dinner that night.
- They express a desire to put the kids to bed with you every night, but more times than not they get caught up watching a game instead and you end up doing it alone.

Red Flag #11: Inflated Sense of Self

Someone with an inflated sense of self thinks they are so good or important that you could not manage without them. They will hold you hostage to their way of doing things because they believe they know best. In conversation with you, they strategically make sure you know you're lucky to have them because you're incapable of doing things as well as they do or that they are the best thing that's ever happened to you. You're the problem, and they're the ultimate solution.

Examples:

- Your coworker refuses to hand off part of a work assignment your boss would like for you to complete, because they don't think you can do it as well as they can.
- The worship leader believes they are so uniquely gifted to play guitar and sing at church that they will not release control of their position and let someone else serve in this way too.
- They sometimes treat you like a child who needs to be bossed around and put in their place.
- They mistreat you and tell you that you need them because "no one else will ever love you like I do."
- They believe they are the better parent and refuse to leave the children in your care until you agree to parent exactly like they do.

Ultimately, we want to see evidence that the people we trust are honest people of integrity, competence, reliability, compassion, good judgment, humility, and stability. But that's not always the case. Sometimes people are unwilling to change or they're living in denial. If a person is living in denial, they are unable or unwilling to see circumstances, relationships, or themselves as they really are. When others try to get involved or share a different perspective, they either back away from the person giving advice or pretend they agree with the wisdom being shared but never take action. So, these red flags help us determine why we may be feeling distrust in our relationships and what issues we need to address.

I don't want to overwhelm you with all these red flags and roots of distrust. But I do want us all to be able to more accurately pinpoint what our concerns are when we are struggling to trust someone. I hope this chapter and the next will help you use more specific and clarifying language when addressing your concerns.

Sometimes we just need help identifying where the real struggle is coming from when we say, "I want to trust you, but I don't." I stayed stuck for so long, not able to verbalize and process what was eating away at me when my feelings of distrust were intense but my words felt vague. After years of working on this for myself, this is what I found to be most helpful in order to say what I needed to say, better understand where the real concerns were coming from, and finally make progress moving forward.

One More Thing I Want You to Know

It's one thing to identify red flags, but it's equally as crucial to assess how serious the red flags are that we are discerning. How big of a deal is this? I've asked this question many times. It's important that we consider several spectrums after we've identified a red flag but before we've made a plan for what to do about it. Assessing red-flag concerns across various spectrums helps you not to just throw out the blanket statement, "I'm struggling to trust you." Instead, you'll be able to talk through these concerns with more specificity and clarity. Process through the following:

- **Spectrum of severity:** Is this critical, significant, problematic, inconvenient, or minor? Remember, every trauma is made up of two parts: fact and impact. When considering the severity, look at both to truly assess how severe this is to you based on your unique wiring, past hurts, and needs/desires.
- **Spectrum of occurrence:** How often is this happening: all the time, sometimes, occasionally, or not often? Is this a consistent pattern or an occasional mistake? The more this happens, the higher the likelihood that your sense of safety with this person will diminish.
- **Spectrum of risk:** How much will this potentially cost you emotionally, financially, mentally, spiritually, or physically? The more intimacy you share with this person, the higher the risk. It is crucial that we count the cost so we understand the short-term and long-term ramifications.
- **Spectrum of proximity:** How often is this person interacting with you? Is this someone you live with and see every day? Is this person someone you interact with daily,

weekly, monthly, or only on occasion? Do you interact with them in person, over the phone, through the internet, or on social media? The more frequently you are with this person, the more their actions will impact you.

- **Spectrum of tolerance:** In this season of your life, how much of this are you willing to tolerate? The scale might look like this: on one end, "I am never okay with this"; in the middle, "I can sometimes tolerate this" or "This rarely bothers me"; and on the opposite end, "This doesn't even show up on my radar."

As you consider red flags in your current and potential relationships, factor in these five spectrums in order to move forward. Don't forget that red flags aren't quite as obvious in newer relationships; it may take some time to pick up on these things. So, give yourself that time. And most of all, be honest about what you are seeing and experiencing.

Remember:

- Red flags we ignore don't typically fix themselves—they just get to be more and more of an issue.
- Discernment is an intimate way God cares for me, leads me, redirects me, warns me, and reveals things to me that I otherwise may miss on my own.
- Safety and connection are directly linked to the health of the trust in a relationship.
- Hyperdesire for safety can mean low levels of connection. Hyperdesire for connection can mean low levels of safety.
- There is a big difference between blind trust and wise trust.

Receive:

"And I pray this: that your love will keep on growing in knowledge and every kind of discernment, so that you may approve the things that are superior and may be pure and blameless in the day of Christ." (Philippians 1:9–10 csb)

"But when he, the Spirit of truth, comes, he will guide you into all the truth. He will not speak on his own; he will speak only what he hears, and he will tell you what is yet to come." (John 16:13)

> "A discerning person keeps wisdom in view,
> but a fool's eyes wander to the ends of
> the earth." (Proverbs 17:24)

"I am sending you out like sheep among wolves. Therefore be as shrewd as snakes and as innocent as doves." (Matthew 10:16)

Reflect:

- Is your heart making excuses or covering up for someone while trying to quiet down the warnings your brain is sending you? What are you saying outwardly that doesn't match what you are feeling inwardly?
- In your own words, what is the difference between blind trust and wise trust? And why is this difference so important?
- What red flags might you be ignoring in your own relationships today?

Pray:

Lord,

I'm asking You for the wisdom and discernment to properly assess red flags I should pay attention to. But first I want to confess that all of us fall short. I have the propensity, just like everyone else, to display some of the behaviors we've looked at in this chapter. Help me not spiral into condemnation of myself or judgment of other people. I want to be harmless as a dove and wise as a serpent (Matthew 10:16). Help me stay in the humble middle. Help me to look at this list in humility and honesty and to let You guide me in what to do next. Help me remember that ultimately my trust needs to be anchored in You and that, as long as I stay near to You, You will give me the discernment I need. Enable me to see what I need to see, hear what I need to hear, know what I need to know, repent of what I need to repent of, and confront what I need to confront.

In Jesus' name, amen.

Chapter Four

Rips and Repairs

•

Isn't it odd that out of the millions of moments we'll experience in a lifetime, most of them will pass without us being able to recall them? These moments become a collective swirl of general memories without a lot of detail. For example, without looking at your phone, what were you doing exactly five months ago today at 2:00 p.m.? What were you wearing? Who were you with? What did you have on your to-do list that day? What made you laugh? What made you cry? What were you stressed about? What did you celebrate? What were you hoping you'd accomplish that day? What prayers did you pray? If it was a normal day, chances are we don't remember.

Doing the math, in my fifty-four years of living, I've experienced over twenty-eight million minutes. My calculator freaked out a bit when I tried to multiply that number by sixty to see how many seconds that equates to. Regardless, it's a lot of moments with countless details that don't register in my memory.

But there are some moments that will stay with me forever. I can recall them with such precision that it's like I'm watching a movie inside my brain. I can tell you the smallest of details without missing a beat. I can feel what I was feeling, especially when the memory is around the unexpected heartbreak of a relationship not being what you once thought it was. And though a lot of healing has happened, I sometimes still find myself a bit stunned by broken trust.

It hurts in ways our hearts weren't designed to hurt. We were made to come together with others, not to be torn apart by others. Broken trust complicates every bit of the parts of love that should be comforting.

I read once that the more intense the emotion is at the time a memory is made, the more likely we are to remember it. That's been so true for me.

One of those moments I think I'll carry forever was the night I knew my marriage was over. I stared at the ceiling, desperate to wake up from this never-ending nightmare. But there would be no waking up from this. There would only be a long road of wading through the debris. Trust had been so severely broken over and over. Even the repair work we'd done now felt futile in light of how everything was turning out.

The wear and tear on all those people who were part of this painful journey had taken its toll. Not only was I losing my marriage, but so many other relationships would also change forever. Even some friendships I thought would stand the test of time had all but disintegrated. Couple friends are complicated when you're no longer a couple. People pick sides. And when they don't know the whole story, you're desperate to tell them. But that's not always possible. People have their reasons and their own issues. People shock you.

Tears leaked from my eyes, but I had no energy to sob like I'd done so many times before. It was like my eyes were purging the last tiny bits of hope I had for this to be turned around. Quietly, one after another, they fell until they stopped.

And then I had the weirdest sensation that this was the moment of transition between the life I'd fought so desperately to keep and the life I would step into where everything was different. I whispered the only prayer I could: "Jesus, I love You, and You love me. That's all I've got."

I wish I could go back in time and tell myself that though the trust in this relationship could not be repaired, other relationships where the trust had been broken would be. Some friends would come back. Family members would too. My kids and I would find our way through the grief of loss. And there would come a day when we would start building a new collection of memorable moments. Good ones we didn't see coming. Indeed, time didn't get stuck in that season of heartbreak. If there is one thing that's true about life after loss, it's that it goes on.

And as time goes on, some relationships will go on with us and some will not.

Some will not, because they walked away.

Some will not, because we made a wise choice to let go.

Some will fade away. As seasons of life change, so do some relationships.

Some will stay as strong as always.

Some will be more complicated and uncertain, because trust has been broken. But perhaps instead of going away, they'll stay. And you'll stay. And now the hard work of repair must begin.

But before we dive into ways to repair trust, let's put some thought into what trust is and how it serves our relationships.

I think the phrase "the ties that bind us" is an accurate picture of human relationships. Trust is made up of incredibly intricate but invisible emotional threads of connection between two people. These threads hold them together. They bring a sense of balance and stability to the relationship. The more the two people honor these threads of trust, the stronger they get. Though neither person can see the threads of trust with their eyes, they feel the strength of their connection in their hearts. The stronger the connection, the more assured both people are in the quality of the relationship.

It feels so fulfilling to be confident you can count on key people you love. I think it's one of the greatest feelings of safety to know that, even if everything else in the world falls apart, you still have a few people who will be right there with you.

But here's the thing no one ever told me. Those few people, that sacred little circle of human connection you think will never change, might not be the same people all the way through life. "Besties for the resties" sounds really good on an Instagram post, but real life doesn't always turn out that way. Promises are sometimes broken. People move away, fade away, pass away, walk away, and turn away. Sometimes there's broken trust. Other times there's just a slow erosion of connection, which diminishes trust. There are also sudden disruptions of trust where they say something you can't unhear, reveal something you can't unknow, or choose something you can't go along with. Or sometimes they withhold information from you, and instead of you being the first to know, you're one of the last.

And certainly there are times when you and I have broken other people's trust. Sometimes we know it. And sometimes we aren't sure what we did. It's good for us to humbly seek clarity. And if there is repair work to be done, and the other person is willing, prayerfully consider what you can do. Let's acknowledge our own imperfections and agree to reread this chapter when we need to make things right with another person.

But for today, let's read this chapter in light of the ways others have broken our trust.

Repairing broken trust requires us to first establish what we need from another person in order to consider them trustworthy. As you read my list, feel free to change it in any way you want, to make it true to what your heart needs to feel safe and secure.

My personal definition of healthy trust with another person means I can count on them . . .

- to be who they say they are;
- to do what they say they are going to do;
- to show up with care and compassion;
- to tell the truth; and
- to use good judgment and biblical wisdom with their decisions.

As I did research by asking others about trust, I found people are unique with their thoughts on what is necessary for someone to be trustworthy in their eyes. Some of the needs are similar to mine but use different wording or are more specific. See if any of these resonate more deeply and need to be on your list of what speaks trustworthiness to you:

- They are authentic.
- They never say, "I probably shouldn't share this, but . . ."
- They show consistency in how they treat you.
- They aren't moody, unpredictable, or prone to angry outbursts.
- They are resourceful.
- You can count on them to be there for you.
- They have longevity in their other relationships.
- They have a good reputation.
- They are loyal.
- They treat all people fairly.
- They are humble enough to admit they are sometimes wrong.
- They are willing to be held accountable.
- They don't dance around issues but instead are straightforward.

- They are available.
- They are cooperative.
- They don't cut corners or cheat.
- They respect other people's property.
- They respect your time.

Good relationships are precious. And just because trust has been broken doesn't mean the relationship is no longer good. Sometimes trust can be diminished even in solid relationships because of missteps like one person not being responsible, not keeping their word, or not showing up with care and compassion like they should have. For me, the biggest determining factor as to whether I'm still safe with a person is how they react to my concerns. I feel more hopeful if they listen without animosity and seek to understand what I need.

My counselor says, "For every rip there needs to be a repair." I really like this advice. If we can address the rips as they happen, it will help us better manage our concerns before they turn into full-blown ruptures. Small breaches of trust are small until they're not. Think of a rope that gets the smallest slice in its side. At first the unraveling doesn't get much notice, until it becomes alarmingly apparent that it could unravel all the way through.

There are also times where we experience much more significant breaches of trust. Bigger betrayals don't just make us pause; they feel like they could possibly take us out. The bigger the rip, the more complicated the repair will be and the longer it will take. The ties that bind us are incredibly strong until they are made fragile because of choices that sliced away at what should have been protected.

Repairing trust that's been more significantly broken can feel daunting. It is hard to figure out where to begin. It's hard to know how to repair what's been cut apart. It's complicated to reattach what was never meant to be severed.

Now, I think it's also important for me to state the obvious here:

there are levels of severity with broken trust. Like I mentioned already, there are rips and there are full-blown ruptures. If you put these two words on opposite ends of a spectrum, you could mark the severity of the broken trust you've experienced. Only you will know how deeply it affected you.

When I started writing this book, I assumed this chapter would be a little more one-size-fits-all. Like, "Here are the things that break trust." And then, "Here are the things that repair broken trust." But how disappointingly unfair it would be for me to assume that giving cookie-cutter answers would suffice. There are many personal factors that make the severity of broken trust unique to you:

- your family-of-origin story
- previous rejections you've experienced
- personal insecurities
- how sentimental you are
- what your priorities are in relationships
- how much this broken trust cost you
- how close you are to this person
- how much it changed the circumstances of your life
- your tolerance level for the poor choices this person made
- whether you believe this breach of trust is a deal-breaker or not

The reason we must first decide how deeply this broken trust impacted us personally, according to our own experiences, is that it is directly linked to the amount of time it will take for the repair. And, even more importantly, it's directly linked to whether you believe repair is even possible.

Low-impact broken trust can likely be repaired with a conversation and a few adjustments. Once those happen, the trust can usually be reestablished and probably even strengthened relatively quickly. Here's why: most of the time, low-impact broken trust is actually a confidence issue and not an integrity issue. For example, I can lose confidence in you because you are forgetful. But forgetfulness isn't usually a breach of honesty, integrity, and character. Broken trust due to a confidence issue is typically categorized as a mistake but not a willful pattern of intentional deception.

But please note that too many rips, even if they are small, without repairs will cause us to lose more and more confidence in someone. When forgetfulness becomes a pattern with no positive progress, the broken trust will start to feel like an integrity issue. That person is no longer just forgetful. They are now becoming a person who doesn't keep their word.

High-impact broken trust will take a lot more time and a lot more work to repair. A friend once told me that in Alcoholics Anonymous there's a saying: "Nine miles in. Nine miles out." This makes me think of the lengths God went to so we would not suffer for all eternity for our sins. The greatest and most significant rip in all of creation is sin. Sin ripped the relationship between God and humanity. If it takes nine miles to get in and nine miles to get out, then in the same sense, this required God to become man in the incarnation to repair the rip of sin. It was mankind who caused the rip. So, as a result, God, through Jesus, was the only one who could repair the relationship and provide a way for deeper intimacy with Him (2 Corinthians 5:18–19).

The deeper the hurt, the longer the journey will be to recovery. No part of repairing severely broken trust should be done quickly. It takes time and believable behavior to establish a new track record.

Don't rush past that. I want this to be one of the statements you forever carry with you: trust takes time plus believable behavior, along with consistency, so a solid track record can be established.

The thing that makes high-impact broken trust take so long to repair is that you're not just having to address the hurtful behavior. The character and integrity issues inside the offender are the real driving force for why the behavior occurred in the first place. Trying to talk through the behavior may address the symptoms, but if their driving force isn't addressed and worked through, it's going to be difficult to rebuild trust with this person. Their choices are most likely an outward sign indicating inward problems that may require specialized therapy. The betrayal trauma they caused you will likely be the result of undealt-with trauma inside them. Again, my counselor wisely taught me, "What people don't work out, they act out." Don't miss this reality.

Even if you've never been made aware of someone else's past traumas, it doesn't mean they don't exist. Honestly, the more I learn about being a human, the more I'm convinced we all have unhealed traumas that can become a driving force for doing things that are hurtful to others. But this should never become an excuse for bad behavior. We are responsible to get the help we need so we don't continue to turn our past hurts into unleashed hurt on the people we do life with. And the person who betrayed you is responsible to get the help they need too.

If the person who betrayed you plays the victim, it's probably not wise to try to rebuild trust with them until their underlying issues are addressed. I know that's a big statement. But it's definitely something that should be factored into this process. And it's not your job to fix them. To see real progress here, you cannot work harder on someone than they are willing to work on themselves.

Now, let's assume the person who broke your trust is willing and able to own the rips they caused and also has a desire to repair them. What do you do next? The first step is to better understand where the breach of trust came from. We started unpacking this in the last chapter, but now, if these red flags have turned into full-blown breaches of trust in your relationship, how can we move forward with repairing? To do that, you'll need to think about what the other person did to break trust with you. Ask yourself, *What is the real issue here?* Not the surface issue or symptom but the roots they've planted in unhealed or unhealthy places of lack that are now causing breaches of trust with you. Below is a list of possible answers to that question, along with the corresponding red flags from the last chapter in parentheses so you can see how red flags can turn into breaches of trust if left un-addressed. Consider, is this breach of trust an issue because of the other person's lack of . . .

- integrity? (immorality, incongruity)
- competence? (incompetence)
- reliability? (irresponsibility, inconsistency)
- care and compassion? (insincerity, self-centeredness)
- good judgment? (insubordination, immaturity)
- humility? (inflated sense of self)
- stability? (insecurity)

In many cases, it will be a combination of several of these. And often when these breaches of trust are combined with a lack of communication, it's like pouring gasoline on a fire—the damage is accelerated.

For the sake of getting started, let's choose the issue that's most alarming to you. Identifying what is lacking in this person that's caus-ing feelings of distrust will help you more clearly define whether this is a high-impact rip or a low-impact rip that needs to be repaired. Again, this is completely up to you to define, based on how the other person's actions affected you.

To some people, a breach of integrity carries the highest impact. To others, they may identify competence as the most damaging breach of trust. This may also change, depending on the type of relationship you have with the person who broke your trust. With your spouse, some of these breaches of trust carry a greater impact on you than a relationship with a coworker would. Regardless, a big part of being able to determine what you need from another person to repair the rip is to identify exactly where the rip came from and how significant the rip is to you.

Before we move on too quickly, I want us to take a collective deep breath. We are dealing with challenging stuff and places of the heart that are tender and may need a moment to sit with what we just read. If we were together right now, I'd say, "Let's go outside and walk for just a bit." If tears need to fall, let them. If you are angry, say it out loud. Here's what I would need: I'd want to look up at the sky and see it's not falling. And I'd want us to whisper to each other, "It's normal to have big feelings around big trust violations. You're okay and so am I."

Once you know the root of the distrust and how significantly this has affected you, the repair work can begin.

Okay, it's time for another list. What I've included on the next page should be a guide, not a checklist. For lower-impact breaches of trust, this list of what you need from the other person can be scaled way back. Not every step will be applicable and necessary. (To help with this, I've put an asterisk next to the steps that may be most appropriate for you to consider with the situation you're facing.)

For higher-impact breaches of trust, this list should help you consider a more comprehensive plan. I recommend working with a counselor or a trusted person who is specifically trained in betrayal trauma as you work through what you're walking through. Don't go at this alone.

Also for higher-impact breaches of trust, it's important to have some trusted friends who will hold private the details of your experience and help you process all the ups and downs of this situation. For me, this was a deeply emotional journey. It wasn't tidy or smooth or without major disappointments. But one thing I held firmly to was that my needs mattered. I had to make sure to weed through the unrealistic needs and expectations I sometimes brought to the table, but I was crystal clear that the other person's willingness to fully participate in this process was crucial. If that was in place, then the other things I needed from them could be worked through.

Again, make this list of needs your own, based on the unique circumstances you have experienced and what will help bring security and trust back into your relationship.

They need to

- fully disclose what they did. Details aren't always helpful (don't go shopping for pain), but be honest about what you need. Disclosed information is so much better than continuously making discoveries of what else happened.
- take responsibility for what they've done.*
- seek to understand how this impacted you.*
- acknowledge what this cost you.
- welcome your questions and desire for clarification.
- give you space and time to grieve if you need to without making you feel guilty, annoying, or weak.
- ask for forgiveness with a truly repentant heart.*
- seek ways to make restitution.*
- establish new patterns in their life that will support them making improvements in this area.*
- stay consistent, so the new patterns become new operating systems for them and eventually become the natural way of doing things.*
- follow through on the small things.
- welcome accountability.
- practice vulnerability.
- tend to their deeper issues with a trained professional, if necessary.
- be willing to go to counseling with you with a heart ready to fully participate.
- be patient with your triggers and ask what you need for reassurance.
- realize the greater the hurt, the longer the healing will take and to be willing to give this the time and attention required.

- be willing to cocreate a new future with you. You'll both have to accept that a repaired relationship will mean a different relationship. Sometimes that means a stronger relationship than before. And other times, different will feel more like meeting someone for the first time, even though you've known them for years.

Remember, this repair work is deeply personal to your unique needs, so take time to consider what will and what will not be restorative for you. Be honest with where you are throughout this process. There will be times you'll need to pull back and take a break. There will be other times you'll want to press in with greater intentionality. Several times throughout my process, I requested that my counselor schedule much longer sessions with me than just one hour. I especially felt this during the disclosure of what happened and how significant the betrayal actually was. I could not work through that on my own. It was crucial when I felt incredibly unsafe and broken that I had the safety net of my counselor's presence and wisdom.

The point is, only you will know what you need and when. Be gentle with yourself and honest with others.

As we wrap up this chapter, I want to remind you of a wonderful gift the Lord has provided for us that will help in this process. The Lord has given us a way to better examine who to trust and what to look for when rebuilding trust. He has told us what it looks like when a person has real evidence of God's Spirit working in them and through them. It's the fruit of the Spirit (Galatians 5:22–25 CSB). Look for the fruit in someone's actions, and you won't have to wade through their words. Anyone can say what you want to hear when rebuilding trust. But the truth comes out in their actions. If their actions are in alignment with the fruit of the Spirit, then most likely Jesus is guiding them. And if Jesus is guiding them, you can trust the good work of Jesus is occurring in them.

Now, you might be asking, Can non-Christians be trustworthy?

Yes, of course. If they have a strong moral compass, then they, too, might show many of these same qualities. But for believers, looking for the fruit of someone's actions is the best way to determine if they are serious about rebuilding that trust. This fruit will produce the believable behavior we've said it takes to determine if it's safe to reestablish a heart connection with this person.

It's normal to be skeptical. And honestly, sometimes it is wise to be skeptical. But skepticism fades in the light of proven truth. How comforting it is to recognize Jesus in a person. When someone consistently produces the fruit of the Spirit over time, they become less mysterious. They will feel less risky. Their presence will feel reassuring. Their absence won't make you afraid of what they might be doing.

> Love replaces selfishness.
> Joy replaces angry outbursts and edgy frustration.
> Peace replaces demands for control.
> Patience replaces a quick temper.
> Kindness replaces rudeness.
> Goodness replaces selfish ambition.
> Faithfulness replaces incessant desire for self-gratification.
> Gentleness replaces a harsh approach.
> Self-control replaces unrestrained impulses.

Instead of constantly feeling tense as you try to figure out if they are being honest with you, evidence of the Spirit will bring reassurance.

Now, what about those people who say they want to rebuild trust with you but have a self-serving agenda? They say with their mouth what you want to hear, but they are still doing things that are off. Or they are still keeping hurtful secrets. They are doing some things right, but there are still a few things that make you feel uneasy. At first, because they're better than they were when things got bad, you assume they are on the right track. But the fruit of the Spirit doesn't get more consistently displayed. Instead, you see those reassuring qualities less and less.

I guess anyone can be an actor and put on a good show. Trust me, I've seen some addicts and some narcissists who deserve an Academy Award. But no show can last forever. They can't hold their breath forever either. With people who pretend to care because it serves them in some way, their reaction to the next time you disappoint them will be very telling.

Eventually, the truth or the lack thereof comes to the surface. What's on the inside of someone always starts to leak out. Even if they seem to be serious this time about reestablishing trust, just a little bit of dishonesty taints

Skepticism fades in the light of proven truth.

their intentions. Even if they tell you several truths and only one lie, deception is like drops of poison—it brings everything they said into question. You will be particularly susceptible to just a little bit of untruth causing big damage when a person is trying to rebuild trust with you.

I once went with a friend whose husband was being given a lie detector test. She and I sat in the lobby waiting for the results. My friend really wanted her husband to pass. She was happy when she found out he was telling the truth on five of the six questions he'd been asked. But then she was confused when the administrator handed her the results, which said her husband was deceptive. She asked him why it seemed the five truthful answers didn't really count and the one question with a deceptive answer made this a failed test. He looked at her with a piercing stare and said, "Your husband is not being truthful with you. End of story."

With this test, each question was crucial. There was no such thing as one little lie. It was the inconsistency that told the administrator everything he needed to know.

There can be grace in this process, but it shouldn't be sloppy grace where deceptions are glossed over.

Again, trust is built through time plus believable behavior. You must have both. And when you have both, a new track record can be established. The longer someone has a consistent track record of trustworthiness, the more credible they'll become and the more you'll finally exhale.

Of course, no one is perfect. There will most likely be missteps in the rebuilding process. However, there really won't be much room for deception. The truth needs to be the truth. And only you know your tolerance for inconsistencies.

Relationships will always carry the risk of pain. Trust is always part risk and part reward. But the more the risks are minimized, the more the rewards are maximized. And with some relationships, there will be the great reward of reestablished trust.

I am so grateful that broken trust doesn't always mean the end of a relationship. It's beautiful when the rips are repaired the right way. And in some cases, because repairs require good communication, those relationships grow stronger. It's much clearer what we each need and desire in the relationship. There's less mystery. There's more vulnerability. And there's a more authentic connection.

I have relationships where this is so wonderfully true. There can be so much joy with relationship restoration. But I also carry the sorrow of other relationships that needed to be released. This journey has shown me I'm stronger than I knew I could be. It has also shown me I have scars that have healed but are so very tender to the touch. My heart is strong and sometimes a little more fragile than it used to be.

Because of what I've been through, I'll probably always have times in my relationships when I have flashes of fear. "What if" questions that pop into my head may make me tense up and momentarily brace myself for heartbreaks unnecessarily. But now I know what to do with all that nervous energy. I don't unleash it on the people I love, unfairly making them pay for the sins of people in my past. I close my eyes and remind myself to relax. I ask myself what is true in that moment and what is not true. I pray and ask for wisdom. I ask for help if I need to process with someone safe. I ask appropriate questions. I look for the fruit or lack thereof. And I lean into the healing and wisdom I've now gained. I got knocked down before, and I may get knocked down again. But one thing I know about myself is that I'm not a girl who stays down.

It reminds me of some advice a skydiving instructor once gave me. (Sidenote: No, I didn't jump out of a plane. But I did defy gravity in a skydiving simulator.) Before I eased my way into the big tube that would blast air up at me, the expert said, "You're going to want to tense up and possibly flail a bit since this is all new to you. But the secret is to relax, straighten your legs, and keep your chin up. When you relax, don't panic if at first you feel like you're sinking too close to the bottom. You may sink a little bit, but then you'll rise." And he was right. My time in that tube wasn't so much about me wanting to be a good indoor skydiver. It was about the victory I experienced when I wanted to panic but didn't. I let my body release all the tension without trying to control anything. I trusted the process and let my body sink. And before I knew it, I did rise.

The sinking was the precursor to rising.

Friend, all those painful memories of broken trust and hurtful deceptions—half-truths, omitted truths, withheld truths, and straight-up lies—will sometimes make their way into your present-day thoughts. Those betrayals will always be part of your past. Remember, they are just a page or possibly a couple of chapters, but that pain is not your full story. You might have had some moments when you did sink, but now it's your time to rise. Here's to better moments and more beautiful memories just waiting to be made.

You might have had some moments when you did *sink*, but now it's your time to *rise*.

One More Thing I Want You to Know

(This is a hard one to read. If you aren't in the mood to read something about relationships that probably won't make it, feel free to skip this one for now.)

There are people who commit life-altering betrayals wrought with ongoing deception, lack of concern for the damage they've caused, and deep-seated character issues that will make trying to repair trust a futile pursuit. It's impossible to repair and build trust that keeps getting broken. If someone hasn't come completely clean about the extent of their betrayal with as full a disclosure as you want, then working on trusting them will just create more and more pain.

I have been in a situation where my desire to save a relationship clouded my judgment on what was honest and what wasn't. The biggest indicator for me that I was trying to give trust to someone who didn't deserve it was that I kept finding out more and more hurtful information. I kept hoping we were making progress, when the truth was, we weren't even at the starting line.

The other indicator that rebuilding trust wasn't going to work with this person was their reaction when I would question something that felt off or triggering to me. Sometimes they were patient with my questions. But other times there was animosity that only made my legitimate and understandable suspicions worse. Statements like "Seriously, you're not over this yet? How much longer am I going to have to answer questions about what I'm doing and where I've been? I'm not doing anything wrong. You're acting crazy."

What I wanted was a statement like "Based on the history

of what happened before, of course that made you nervous when I wasn't where I said I would be. What do you need from me right now for reassurance? Let's get you the facts you need to feel assured. And let's make a game plan so this doesn't happen again."

Without compassion, honesty, humility, and true repentance on the part of the offender, broken trust will most likely stay broken. Trust requires both parties to be willing to work through the process of rebuilding.

There will be times we have hoped for a person to be what we want them to be. We've waited for them to become trustworthy. We've given it our all, but sometimes it's too much allowance. We wrongly think forgiveness means going back to them and their behavior. We hope. We keep giving them chances. *This time they will be someone I can trust.* But their actions, over and over, tell us they are not trustworthy. At some point, instead of listening to their empty promises, we have to listen to the message they are sending with their actions.

I think we, as Christian women, feel an enormous pressure to show our forgiveness is real by continuing to stay in this relationship no matter what. But God is not honored when you are being treated in dishonorable and deplorable ways. We've been taught that our love should be unconditional, but reconciling with someone who has broken our trust in the deepest ways should absolutely be conditional. Conditions like whether they are repentant, getting the help they need, being held accountable, and so forth. These should all be put in place for the sake of your safety, stability, sanity, and dignity.

Remember, sometimes distrust is the only responsible trust there is. Distrust in situations of continued broken trust is not a sign of weakness. It's a sign of great strength.

Remember:

- Broken trust complicates every bit of the parts of love that should be comforting.
- Skepticism fades in the light of proven truth.
- You might have had some moments when you did sink, but now it's your time to rise.
- God is not honored when you are being treated in dishonorable and deplorable ways.
- Distrust in situations of continued broken trust is not a sign of weakness. It's a sign of great strength.

Receive:

"All this is from God, who reconciled us to himself through Christ and gave us the ministry of reconciliation: that God was reconciling the world to himself in Christ, not counting people's sins against them. And he has committed to us the message of reconciliation." (2 Corinthians 5:18–19)

"But the fruit of the Spirit is love, joy, peace, patience, kindness, goodness, faithfulness, gentleness, and self-control. The law is not against such things. Now those who belong to Christ Jesus have crucified the flesh with its passions and desires. If we live by the Spirit, let us also keep in step with the Spirit." (Galatians 5:22–25 CSB)

Reflect:

- Considering what the other person did to break trust with you, ask yourself, *Is this breach of trust an issue because of their lack of*
  - » integrity?
  - » competence?
  - » reliability?
  - » care and compassion?
  - » good judgment?
  - » humility?
  - » stability?
- How would your outlook on life and relationships change if you were to apply the steps on pages 66–67 each time there's a rip or rupture that needs a repair?

Pray:

God,

Help me see that not every mistake someone makes is a breach of trust. Give me wisdom and grace with this. Also, help me to not gloss over the rips that need repair. Thank You for walking this path alongside me and for healing my heart in the ways You have. It comforts me to know You deeply understand the pain of betrayal and hurt I've been experiencing. Give me the courage and patience to see my circumstances for what they are and what I need to move forward. Comfort my heart when the way seems impossible. You are my steady place.

In Jesus' name, amen.

Chapter Five

And I Didn't Want to Be Alone

•

As the months turned into years after my divorce, the number one question I got was "When are you going to start dating?" *Dating*. That felt like such an awkward word to me. Dating? Me? I'm a mom of five grown children. I'm a grandmother. I'm a Bible teacher. I was married for almost thirty years. And then suddenly I wasn't.

I didn't want to try again.
And I didn't want to be alone.
I didn't want to risk being hurt again.
And I didn't want to be alone.
I didn't want to be so closely connected to another man that his choices, which I have no say in, could unleash devastating consequences in my family's life.
And I didn't want to be alone.

I didn't want to engage in the level of trust required for
    romantic closeness.
And I didn't want to be alone.
I didn't want to share my closet again.
And I didn't want to be alone.

In theory, I knew I wasn't *alone* alone. I had very close relationships with my people. I had a solid tribe, and I knew there were people I could count on. But there were some moments when I felt so intensely alone, it was physically painful.

I felt lost in my aloneness. I felt odd, sad, awkward, and like I didn't quite fit into the life we'd previously built as a couple.

Alone doesn't just happen when there's no one around. Sometimes *alone* means you're carrying the weight of something hard by yourself. People around you are supportive. But they can't truly understand the gravity of what it feels like to be you. They can't understand the full weight of being a single parent, taking on all of the bills and other responsibilities that used to be shared.

People genuinely care, but who wants to always hear a sad answer every time they ask, "How are you?" At some point, I just started saying I was good, because every other answer sounded like a pitiful broken record. I knew people weren't pitying me, but constantly talking about my hardships made me feel small, incapable, and like the sum total of my life was the fallout from this divorce. Plus, some of their suggestions weren't realistic. And sometimes their thoughts on what I should do felt void of a true understanding of how very broken my heart was. It's hard to rally and just get on with things when every move you make feels so very risky, like you're navigating a foreign land with no map and no guide. And with the intense fear of others judging you for not taking their advice.

Sometimes it just feels safer to keep your thoughts to yourself. And when you don't have someone to process this stuff with, *alone*

It's hard to rally and just

get on with things when

every move you make

feels so *very risky*.

means a whole lot of hard thoughts and questions and fears staying all tangled up inside you. If you go to bed with confusing thoughts, you'll wake up with confusing emotions. And you can quickly spiral without someone to bring balance and assurances.

This aloneness wasn't just with my thoughts. It also played out with physical safety. When you're alone, there's no one to help you decide if the strange noise you heard in the middle of the night warrants a call to the police. If you dare to check and see what it is, you're doing that on your own. You're shaking, but last time it was just a branch that was tapping your window. It's probably something like that again, but what if it's not? Aloneness can be scary.

Also, when the person who was the closest to you is suddenly no longer there, you get caught off guard by how much the world expects you to have someone you can count on if something happens to you. I remember the first time I was filling out some paperwork that required me to list my emergency contact. My chest tightened. My stomach clenched. I'd lost my emergency contact. To everyone else filling out paperwork in the doctor's office that day, it was just another annoying form attached to a clipboard. To me, it was another shock. Another loss. Another wave of grief.

And then there was a vacation with beautiful scenery. I wound up being the photographer for all the couples who were on the trip with me. In the few pictures I had them take of just me, I looked like I had forgotten how to stand normally and my stiff hands had no clue where to go.

Then there was the RSVP situation. Which is the lesser of two difficult choices? Should I check "plus one," knowing good and well that chances were almost 100 percent that I'd be attending alone? Or should I just state I'd be coming alone, which felt like an intense way to once again announce I was the divorced friend?

I was surrounded by couples. And I loved that until it hurt. I started to feel like the little corner of the world I lived in was built for couples—two people who go together, sit together, stand together, travel together, pose together, arrive together, and leave together.

"A table for two?" every restaurant hostess would ask.

"No, just one. Just me." There were times this was okay. But then there were times where this was a reminder of a huge loss in my life. My ex had already moved on and there was another woman sitting in the seat I used to occupy across from him.

I no longer wanted to be in that seat, but it still felt shocking. Others felt it, too, and offered sweet sentiments that should have made me feel seen but instead made me feel weird.

"My heart breaks for you."

"Please know I'm praying for you often."

"I can't imagine how hard this is."

There is nothing wrong with these statements. I'm sure I've said versions of these same well-meaning sentences to others. It's just that I was already feeling like somehow this divorce had not just made me feel intensely alone but had also diminished who I was and how people saw me. And maybe most tragic, how I saw myself. I wanted to shake loose the word *divorced* from my life. But there it was every new day.

So, back to the most dreaded question of all: "When are you going to start dating?"

The thought of adding dating into this mix? No, thank you! The risk of getting my heart and my trust broken again? No, thank you! The fear of adding more drama and more dysfunction and more reasons for people to feel sorry for me? Absolutely not.

My decision not to date was multifaceted. But if I'm really honest about it, dating felt like inviting people close who would be highly unpredictable.

I knew if someone else got close enough to be known as my new person, I couldn't control life nearly as much as I wanted to. When we have our trust broken, it's tempting to replace trust with control. If I can control it, I don't have to deal with my trust issues. And when I say "control," I mean "do everything I can to keep things as predictable as possible." If I can stay in control of situations, then I falsely believe I can avoid the risk of trust.

I realize your next step forward may not be in the dating arena, but this plays out in other ways as well. At work, I don't have to trust that someone will do their job if I am micromanaging their tasks. In my friendships, I don't have to trust that I won't get disappointed or be a disappointment to someone if I keep our conversations from getting too deep and only get together with them occasionally. However this translates into your fears around trust, I want to validate how scary it can feel to trade the predictability we want for the risk of relationships with no guarantees.

I wanted what felt predictable so badly that I was willing to miss out on all that might be possible.

I thought, *If I can't control the risk, I can't engage with a relationship in any kind of depth.* Sometimes it is smart not to have deep conversations when we are dealing with people we can't remove from our lives but who have proven themselves untrustworthy. But it's not smart when this becomes our thinking around everyone. Then we find ourselves trying to control the narrative in all our relationships, using arm's-length statements like:

"This opportunity sounds good, but honestly I'm not even sure I want it."
"He sounds like a great guy, but I'm just not sure I'm interested."
"I'd like to get to know that person better, but I've got a lot on my plate right now."
"I know we are supposed to do this project together, but I just went ahead and did most of it since I had the time."

Those all sound like reasonable responses, but are they really true? Sometimes I would act like I didn't want something or that I'd prefer to do it alone, rather than risk more disappointment. However, if what I'm saying on the outside doesn't match what I'm feeling on the inside, then I may be trying to control the situation and the narrative around it. Or at least give the illusion that I'm in control. In a later chapter we are going to dig deeper into what to do when a lack of trust makes us want more control. But for now let's just acknowledge it's really hard to trust someone new when doing so could cause us to feel subject to a situation we can't control.

I told everyone around me I would never consider dating again. Dating felt like a huge leap into an unknown that terrified me. But each time I said never, something would flinch inside me. I had desires that conflicted with my "never" statement. My refusal made me feel in control, which felt great . . . until those moments when I longed for someone to love me again. I had even declared "no dating for me" on a popular podcast after I'd been single for nearly two years. Then the gal interviewing me suddenly turned the interview from me giving advice to me receiving advice. She was so loving and had me crying by the end of the interview. I still couldn't wrap my head around the possibility of dating. But there was something this podcaster said that wouldn't leave me. The theme of her advice to me was this: "It's never too late."

I had somehow bought into the notion that the end of my marriage meant the end of me ever feeling truly loved. Truly treasured. Truly chosen. I guess as a Bible teacher I'm supposed to say God is the one who makes all of this true for me. Yes, I agree. And my heart also longed for this from a man too.

My podcaster friend's "never too late" statement stuck to me. Hung on to me. Sometimes felt annoyingly glued to my thoughts. Never. Too. Late. Ugh.

The minute I could admit that I did desire to be loved by someone, my fears around trust made me quickly exhale and shake my head. After enough time had passed so people wouldn't connect the dots, the podcaster gave her listeners updates on her hopes for me by calling me "Never Too Late." It was weird to listen to her podcast and know she was secretly referring to me. But it was also comforting to have someone believe in good possibilities for me.

She didn't pity me. She didn't pressure me. But she also didn't play along with my plan to reduce my possibilities for the future to only what I could control. She just kept reminding me there was more to my life than what I could see for myself.

It's good to have at least a few friends who are bold enough to pray big prayers and see big things for you. But when you are healing from a broken heart and broken trust, it's really important that these are friends who are also wise enough not to put undue pressure on you and who still let you walk through your process. I felt safe enough with my "never too late" friend to let her have dreams for me that I wouldn't allow myself to have.

Another one of my friends, Mel, wrote in her journal what she clearly felt God was showing her about my future. One night we were playing cards on my back patio, and I told her, "I think I'm going to be alone the rest of my life. I don't think I can risk getting hurt again." Mel listened without interrupting as I continued. "Maybe, over time, I'll get used to being single. I mean, one cool thing is I won't have to share my closet."

I smiled. And then my smile started quivering until the tears rolled down my face. No more words would come out. It's hard to move forward when what I really want is something from my distant past. Something that I can't reach. That I can't touch. But that is still very alive in my memories.

In my case, I didn't want to get back the person in my past. I wanted to get back the innocent thoughts I once had about my marriage. I wanted to get back the feeling of knowing I had a person. I wanted to get back the feeling that I could trust a person to have my best interests in mind. I wanted to get back the feeling of safety that what this person had invested in our life together was enough that they'd protect our vision because they wanted it as much as I did.

Of course, my memories from back then probably contained more ideas of how I wanted things to be than how they actually were. But still, the pictures in my mind were of a time when I felt more confident about what my future would look like.

Now, it was like I was constantly turning corners without any clue whether I was going to feel good about what I saw or terrified of what was waiting for me.

Mel said, "You are in a good place. You've done so much healing work. You have processed and prayed and spent time in counseling. You've taken time. I know you enough to know that this one sad night is not what I've been seeing the past two years. You are no longer consumed with the past. You used to talk about what happened over and over with me. But you're not there anymore. I see you looking forward with joy, laughter, and hope. I think you are ready to date. And what I feel like God showed me was that it won't be much longer for you."

Nothing changed for another long stretch of time. I didn't have an epiphany that suddenly made me courageous enough to open up more possibilities for my future. I didn't turn some big corner where I realized controlling isn't a good long-term replacement for trusting. I didn't wake up one day with a neon sign telling me I was ready to start dating.

My friends thought I was ready. My counselor thought I was ready. But I wouldn't believe it for myself until I took a step. A baby step. A small declaration step where I stopped letting my fears hold me back, where I stopped doubting my own discernment. Sometimes when you get shockingly bad results from past decisions, it can make you hesitant to trust that you're capable of making wise future decisions. Trusting myself to call out concerns and not look past them or feel pressured into thinking I'm making a big deal out of nothing was a mistake I didn't want to repeat. Could I trust myself to see things more clearly? To name what I saw? To choose not to wait until a red flag was a full-on fire before calling it red? I wasn't sure. And I never would be sure as long as I was trying to analyze my readiness. I would have to try it inside the context of real life with real people.

So the first baby step I took was to stop using the term "never." This wasn't a step into a relationship. Not a step into declaring I was ready to trust someone. Not a step into saying I was even ready for dating. Just a baby step toward being open to the possibility. And a baby step away from doubting myself.

Sometimes when you get shockingly bad results from past decisions, it can make you hesitant to trust that you're capable of making wise future decisions.

Ironically enough, I was with Mel again one random afternoon when another friend texted me and said, "No pressure at all, but would you ever consider going out with a friend of my husband? Great guy. Loves Jesus."

I laughed, read her the text, and immediately started typing back a polite refusal.

Mel kindly and softly said, "Lysa, maybe this is a good, safe baby step. Maybe it will be wonderful, and you'll feel a peace from God and a sense that *Yes, this is the right first step.* Or maybe it will be awful, and you'll know this isn't right for right now. Or maybe it will be somewhere in between, where you aren't sure and you just need time to figure out if this is right for you."

I gripped my chair. Mel continued. "You don't have to make any big decisions about trust right now. You don't have to decide if you are willing to risk giving your heart to someone and jumping into the deep end of a relationship. Just take one step toward moving forward."

That was the shift I needed. I didn't have to define my future in order to step into the future. I didn't have to decide if dating was going to be part of the plan or not. But I also didn't need to limit what the future could look like.

No matter how good my illusions of keeping myself safe by trying to stay in control seem, they don't work. The future is coming whether I want it to or not. And the future, just like the present, will have a whole lot that is completely out of my control.

It's like when I was a little girl and I got scared of getting off the escalator. To my little eyes, the sharp edges, disappearing into the place where I was supposed to get off, looked like monster teeth. So I started going back up the forward-moving stairs. But as I went up and the stairs kept going down, I couldn't keep up. It was forcing me forward. It was way riskier to have the escalator force me off the end than for me to just step off the end. I was afraid, but still I stepped off. And I didn't get eaten by the monster teeth. There was no monster. All I had to do was take one step.

And so I did. It wasn't all rosy and wonderful. But it also wasn't all horrible and treacherous. Bonus: I didn't freak out or pass out. I just put one foot in front of the other. And the rhythm of moving forward actually felt way more empowering than I ever thought possible.

One More Thing I Want You to Know

Can I trust this person? is a big question. The more we feel pressured, internally or externally, to give a definitive answer, the riskier the outcome will feel. How can you know that someone who has broken your trust is now at a place to be responsible with your trust? It will take time. Remember, the bigger the betrayal, the longer the repair will take.

How can you know if a new person in your life is trustworthy? That will also take time.

How do you know you can trust yourself to properly discern trustworthiness when you've gotten it wrong before or were made to feel crazy for asking questions when things didn't make sense? Again, it will all take time.

But time itself isn't enough. Just to reiterate, building or rebuilding trust requires a combination of three things: time, believable behavior, and a track record of trustworthiness. Taking baby steps allows for all three of those things to happen.

In my own life, I knew if I was going to be able to reengage with people who had broken my trust in the past or if I was going to consider a new relationship, it wasn't going to happen overnight. I also knew if I was going to learn to trust my own ability to have wise discernment and reestablish my confidence to hear from the Lord, it would need to happen slowly. Isaiah 30:19–21 has been such a comfort for me as I take these baby steps toward trust:

> People of Zion, who live in Jerusalem, you will weep no more. How gracious he will be when you cry for help! As soon as he hears, he will answer you. Although the Lord gives you the bread of adversity and the water of affliction, your teachers will be hidden no more; with your own eyes you will see them. Whether you turn to the right or to the left, your ears will hear a voice behind you, saying, "This is the way; walk in it."

The principle of these verses is that God does respond to us when we cry out to Him. The "right and left" mentioned mean, as long as you stay within the will and command of God, you're headed in His direction and you're going to hear Him. He will guide you. In other words, the goal is to live a life of congruity where our life lines up with God's Word.

But what about the slowness of this whole trust process? What about how painful it can be in the waiting to see if someone is trustworthy or not?

The historical context of these verses gives me great comfort in the face of these understandable questions. Isaiah was addressing the Israelites in a season of waiting. The idea is that waiting can be lonely, and at times we can feel defeated. Waiting can also make us feel incredibly anxious when there are so many unknowns. But remember this: whenever we are waiting *on God*, we are actually waiting *with God*. The fact that the Teacher is behind us brings to mind the nearness of God. One Old Testament scholar said it this way: "A word behind you conveys both the nearness of God and the sensitivity of the pupil."[12]

When I asked my friend Dr. Joel Muddamalle about these verses, he said, "The attentive nature of the follower of God who desires to be led by God is important here. The New Testament develops this further with the concept of the Spirit-filled life of believers. We are led by the Spirit not based on our own ambition but by the vision and direction of God" (Galatians 5:16–25 and John 16:13).

And if we get it wrong by turning left or right outside of God's will? When this takes place, God will call out and get us back on track. One of the things that is often overlooked is the fact that Isaiah didn't expect perfection. He assumed there would be moments of error, times when we would go astray—but when that happens, as long as our hearts are willing to receive correction, we can be sure God will redirect us.

Remember:

- When we have our trust broken, it's tempting to replace trust with control.
- *Alone* doesn't just happen when there's no one around. Sometimes *alone* means you're carrying the weight of something hard by yourself.
- It's hard to rally and just get on with things when every move you make feels so very risky.
- It can be scary to trade the predictability we want for the risk of relationships with no guarantees.
- Sometimes when you get shockingly bad results from past decisions, it can make you hesitant to trust that you're capable of making wise future decisions.

Receive:

"People of Zion, who live in Jerusalem, you will weep no more. How gracious he will be when you cry for help! As soon as he hears, he will answer you. Although the Lord gives you the bread of adversity and the water of affliction, your teachers will be hidden no more; with your own eyes you will see them. Whether you turn to the right or to the left, your ears will hear a voice behind you, saying, 'This is the way; walk in it.'" (Isaiah 30:19–21)

"But when he, the Spirit of truth, comes, he will guide you into all the truth. He will not speak on his own; he will speak only what he hears, and he will tell you what is yet to come." (John 16:13)

Reflect:

○ Does the slowness of the process of trusting someone feel difficult for you? Why do you think that is?
○ "The bigger the betrayal, the longer the repair will take." How does this statement sit with you, and have you found it to be true in your life?

Pray:

Lord,

You know my desire to have close relationships based on truth and goodness. You also see my tendency to try to control my circumstances and the people around me when things look scary and unknown because of what I've been through. Help me step forward as the healed version You see in me—the one You're making me into. This feels messy and unpredictable, but I know I can trust You and the ways You are working on me and for me.

I pray all of this in Jesus' name, amen.

Chapter Six

How Can I Trust God When I Don't Understand What He Allows?

·

There's a lot I don't understand. I don't understand why good relationships sometimes go very, very badly. I don't understand why two people can look at the exact same situation and have two completely different interpretations of what happened. I don't understand why a friend you've trusted for years would suddenly unleash a tremendous amount of pain and devastation by turning on you. I don't understand why a family member you share the greatest amount of history with, a connection that goes DNA deep, would suddenly do something so shocking that you can no longer trust them. I don't understand why people who seem so good would turn out to be those you never should have trusted.

I wouldn't have treated them that way.

And there it is . . . the statement that makes me want to pull away as distrust sets in.

I wouldn't have done what they did.

I wouldn't have sent such a scathing email.

I wouldn't have accused my friend before getting the facts straight.

I wouldn't have assumed a friend had terrible motives when her track record shows she has a good heart.

I wouldn't have just failed to show up when I knew someone was counting on me.

I wouldn't have turned on them like they turned on me.

I wouldn't have taken what wasn't mine.

I wouldn't have cheated, lied, or betrayed them.

I wouldn't have talked about them in such harsh ways.

Or at least I'm pretty sure I wouldn't have done what they did. Of course, but for the grace of God, I could do a lot of stuff I never thought I would do. But these scripts of "I would never do that" aren't just about the actions of other people. These thoughts carry over into my thoughts about God.

I wouldn't have written the story like this. I wouldn't have allowed that to happen. I wouldn't have put those I love through so much suffering. I wouldn't have waited so long. I wouldn't have seemed so silent.

What my mind can't understand, my heart tends to distrust. When I can't understand what God is allowing or I feel confident He will do something and it doesn't happen, doubts can easily turn into distrust.

I'm realizing that I attach a great deal of my trust in God to my desire for things to turn out like I think they should. I want the goodness of God to compel Him to fix things, change minds, prevent hurt, punish the bad, and vindicate the good on my timeline. I want the goodness of God to make people who do hurtful things say they are sorry and then act better, do better, be better. I'm desperate for Him to make circumstances good. To ensure that churches are good. To intervene in relationships and make them good. To provide jobs and

What my *mind* can't understand,

my *heart* tends to distrust.

finances and other things that make us feel secure, in the timing that seems good to me.

I want the goodness of God to make life good right now. I want the goodness of God to mean that things turn out okay according to my definition of okay-ness. I want the goodness of God to work like a fair transaction: do good things and good things will happen to me.

I know the goodness of God means God is good even when everything else isn't. But I have such a hard time with this. Especially when there's a lot of pain in the waiting for God's goodness to be revealed.

I will have to trust God with what I cannot see. I will have to trust God with what I do not know. I will have to trust God with what I fear. I will have to trust God with what I want and, even more so, with what I do not want. I might have to bear what I desperately do not want to bear. I may have to face what I desperately do not want to face. I may have to go through what I desperately do not want to go through.

God is good. I know this. But when the pain and suffering get intense, I sometimes feel less and less certain that His goodness will come through for me. That's not fun to confess. But confessing it is better than continuing to do what I've been doing for a long time: pretending these thoughts aren't there or shaming myself for thinking such things.

I don't want to seem ungrateful, not grounded enough in Scripture, or disappointing to others who expect me to be more mature in my faith. It's not that I'm losing faith in God. It's that I'm having to learn faith requires trust in Him. I will have to walk a path while not seeing where it will go or knowing how long it will be. A path where I fear the hardships may crush me.

My struggle is this: Can I trust Him enough to *really* start surrendering the outcomes . . . the plans . . . the way my life will go?

Proverbs 3:5–6 instructs, "Trust in the LORD with all your heart and lean not on your own understanding; in all your ways submit to him, and he will make your paths straight." I know these verses.

I want to live these verses. Not just quote this but truly live this. But in order to do that, I must acknowledge God's version of making my path straight most likely will not line up with what I expect. He may have a completely different definition of *straight*. Another way to understand *straight* is that God is able to see into the future and to make sense of it. My understanding will never allow for this. So I must submit to Him the way I think things should go. And then trust Him enough to walk in His way.

Can I do that? Can I make peace with the fact that my definition of a path being made straight is limited by my human thinking and human emotion? Can I find my security in the unlimited, all-knowing power of God?

I'm not asking you to confess anything here. But see if you relate to any of the following thoughts about trusting God when you're hurting and confused about what is happening:

- How could God have watched that person do such hurtful things and not have stopped it?
- I've been believing God will bring good from this, but the good never seems to come.
- When good things do happen, I feel like it's part of God's redemption. But then when another hurtful or confusing turn of events happens, it feels cruel that God provided just enough good to get my hopes up, only to watch it all fall apart again.
- I say with my mouth all the Christian versions of how good God is, but deep in my heart I'm full of questions that don't seem appropriate to ask.
- Sometimes what I say about how much I trust God is so incongruent with the pain and disappointment inside me that it makes me feel like I'm not being honest.
- I feel confused when it seems like God is coming through for me but not for my friend, who I've prayed and prayed for. It

makes me feel guilty and like I'm abandoning her in the pain we once shared together.

- I'm tired of relationships and circumstances being so complicated and challenging. People know I trust God, but all this stuff that keeps happening makes following God look less and less appealing, and I don't know what to say in response to their doubt. It's especially difficult when I have lots of doubts as well.

I don't feel these things all the time. But at different points in my journey, these thoughts have bored into the deepest and most vulnerable part of me. And before long, I've felt like I had more faith in my fears coming true than in God coming through for me.

> *Sometimes I can have more faith in my fears coming true than in God coming through for me.*

I imagine my insides being hollowed out like a big, uprooted oak tree I once saw after some bad weather. It was a stately tree that appeared incredibly grounded and stable. But as I got closer to the fallen giant, I saw that when it fell, the roots were so shallow they lifted out of the ground as well. I also noticed, as a crew was cutting up the tree to remove it, the tree was hollow on the inside. So I walked over to some of the men working on it. I just had to know: What made such a seemingly immovable tree fall?

One of the men said, "Shallow roots and ants."

I tilted my head and betrayed the fact that I communicate for a living. "Huh?" I replied.

He went on to explain that sometimes big trees that grow in yards with sprinkler systems get so easily satisfied by the water from the surface that the roots don't need to go deep into the ground for water. The trees can look strong and stable, but shallow roots make them less stable and way more vulnerable in storms and strong winds.

Oh boy. I could feel the life lesson coming in hot. When life pretty much looks like I expect it to and feels relatively good, I am tempted to get satisfied with where I am and not continue to grow deeper and deeper in my faith. Or if I'm just letting others sprinkle some biblical wisdom on me through their sermons and podcasts but I'm not digging into God's Word and going deeper in my application, then my roots will be shallow. That all seems okay until a storm comes. And storms always eventually do come.

But shallow roots aren't the only reason this tree fell.

The ants played a big part as well. They target a tree where some sort of injury has occurred and the moisture that gets in has started to weaken the wood. The ants take full advantage of the softer wood and wear away at it, eventually even damaging the sound wood and making the tree hollow inside, even though it may look solid from the outside. The more hollow the tree becomes, the more it will lose structural strength.

Whew, another life lesson. Each time I have doubts and fears about God's goodness, I need to bring these to God. I need to create a sacred space with God and His Word to wrestle and cry and trust Him with my doubts. But I don't always do that. Left unattended, these doubts and questions start to frame the way I look at things. The more uncertain I am about what God is or is not doing right now, the more resistant I am to trusting Him with my future.

Sometimes the pain of today feels like a declaration of what my whole future will look like. These thoughts don't seem like that big of a deal one by one—just like you would never look at an ant and think it could possibly take down a huge oak tree. Please hear me: it's not wrong to have these thoughts, but it is dangerous to get consumed by them. To get hollowed out by them. To get even more vulnerable to the storms around us because of thoughts that erode our only true stability.

Each doubt we have will cause us to either press into God or pull away from Him.

We press into Him by doing what we already know to do: get into His Word, pray, listen to Him, look for evidence of His goodness, and remember times when He was faithful in the past. That's what I should do. And it's often what I will do with situations that won't cost me much. But when it's a situation where a whole lot of fear and emotion are involved and nothing seems to be working out, I want a more immediate relief to my pain and more visible evidence that this is all going to work out in a way that seems good to me. I don't want to imagine a future where I lose another relationship or another thing that helps me feel secure.

And all the Bible study girls who are barely holding it together under the weight of broken hearts, broken friendships, broken dreams, and broken trust say, "True that. Same with me."

If I don't feel like God is coming through for me today, it's so hard to trust that surrendering my future to Him is a safe thing to do. I'm scared to fully trust Him. I'm scared to fully surrender my efforts to fix things and instead cling to His promises. So I hold on to my fears and doubts, and I build safety nets in case He doesn't come through.

For me, safety nets come in many different forms. Sometimes I will hold back from verbalizing what I really want so I don't feel so disappointed or look dumb when it doesn't happen. Or I try to force things to happen in my way and in my time, because I'm just so tired of waiting on God. Or I do everything I think I should to please God, hoping my goodness will convince Him I deserve the outcome I really want. (Insert me rolling my eyes at myself.) Or, like an ostrich with its head stuck in the sand, I deny what I'm really feeling because I would rather numb out or live in denial than do the hard work of acknowledging my struggles with trusting God. Or lastly, I blame people for why things aren't turning out like I think they should, as if the people who have broken my trust somehow had the ability to thwart God's plans.

I'm not saying you do any of these things. But if you relate on any level, take a deep breath.

Of course, trusting God can be a real struggle sometimes. Hebrews 11:1 teaches us, "Now faith is confidence in what we hope for and assurance about what we do not see." Specifically, this verse is talking about salvation and the assurance that Jesus has risen from the grave and will return for us. Early Christians were discouraged and needed to remember the faith stories of those who had gone before them. And today I have confidence and assurance that God has already come through for me from an eternal perspective through Jesus being my Savior. However, I struggle having confidence and assurance that God is going to come through for me on this side of eternity. I love how theologian F. F. Bruce explained this: "Physical eyesight produces a conviction or evidence of visible things; faith is the organ which enables people to see the invisible order."[13]

I don't always want to leave room for the mystery of God. I want faith to operate with the speed of my eyesight. Like when I say, "I hope my keys are on the counter," and all I have to do is look at the counter for physical confirmation that the keys are there. I am desperate for visible evidence, so faith doesn't feel so risky.

Why would I admit all of this to you? Because I want this to be a safe place to process. And I've come to the realization that this kind of wrestling isn't bad or ungodly. Actually, the first step toward learning how to surrender to God's version of good and trust Him with all of our hearts is acknowledging our struggle. If we want to change our reality, then we have to start by admitting our reality. And I think I'm exhausted enough to finally want to learn to live the reality of truly trusting God.

Sit with that for a minute.

What if a big part of our exhaustion and anxiety around hard circumstances is that we are constantly trying to remove faith from our relationship with Him? When we trust people, we are looking for evidence we can see with our physical eyes that trusting them is safe. Faith doesn't work that way. Faith will always make us anxious and unsure unless we are confident in the goodness of God. If we stand firm on His goodness and know everything He allows is somehow flowing from that goodness, then we will have a lot less fear in trusting Him. Faith in God means to be assured of His goodness even when what He allows doesn't feel good, seem good, or look good right now. Faith is our confidence in what we hope for. Faith is our assurance about what we do not see.

There will always be a gap between what we see and the full story God knows. That gap is where so many of my fearful "what if" questions come from as I look ahead and play out worst-case scenarios.

But let's flip that. Let's think through some what-if questions that point us toward God's goodness instead of all the doubts that point us toward distrust. You may find it helpful to use a journal as you take time to fill in these blanks and write any additional thoughts you have. We will start with honest admissions about why it's hard for us to trust God sometimes. But keep going. The whole exercise in this next section is leading somewhere good.

For our first what-if question, let's address the fears tangled around our faith.

What if I wrote down each thought of distrust so they don't stay all jumbled up inside me as a big feeling of fear and anxiety?

- I fear trusting God with _____, because He allowed _____ to happen in my past.
- I fear trusting God with _____, because if He doesn't come through for me in the way I want Him to, I will suffer _____.
- I fear trusting God with _____, because I don't think God will really _____.
- I fear trusting God with the suffering and heartbreak I'll go through if _____ happens, and I fear I won't ever _____.

What if expressing my true feelings to God is a beautiful act of trusting God?

I recently received an email from a friend who was helping me process expressing to God what I really feel. She said, "I'm reminded of a quote sometimes attributed to Sigmund Freud: 'Unexpressed emotions will never die. They are buried alive, and will come forth later, in uglier ways.' The more I tried to bury my doubts, the uglier the doubts became. Acknowledging them instead of stuffing them down brought healing and new growth." How does this tie into trust? Well, verbalizing my doubts to Him is an expression of trust in God. If I can trust God with doubts about Him, then I can trust Him with anything.

Try writing a little more. Fill in these blanks:

- I sometimes doubt that God will _____, because _____.
- I feel _____ right now because God is (or isn't) doing _____.
- What I really want to see happen is _____. And if this doesn't happen, it will cause me to feel _____.
- I don't want to feel _____, because I don't think I could handle _____.

What if I looked at Scripture in a new way?

Too often, I read God's Word to try to make sense of what I'm facing. But what if the Scriptures are really inviting us to see in part how God sees things?

Read through the following verses, and journal about those that help you see a little more of what God sees. How does that comfort you? And what part of this still concerns you?

- "I will instruct you and teach you in the way you should go; I will counsel you with my loving eye on you." (Psalm 32:8)

- "The LORD does not look at the things people look at. People look at the outward appearance, but the LORD looks at the heart." (1 Samuel 16:7)
- "Your Father knows what you need before you ask him." (Matthew 6:8)
- "May the God of hope fill you with all joy and peace as you trust in him, so that you may overflow with hope by the power of the Holy Spirit." (Romans 15:13)
- "'For My thoughts are not your thoughts, nor are your ways My ways,' says the LORD. 'For as the heavens are higher than the earth, so are My ways higher than your ways, and My thoughts than your thoughts.'" (Isaiah 55:8–9 NKJV)
- "And do not be conformed to this world, but be transformed by the renewing of your mind, so that you may prove what the will of God is, that which is good and acceptable and perfect." (Romans 12:2 NASB)
- "If our hearts condemn us, we know that God is greater than our hearts, and he knows everything." (1 John 3:20)

What if, instead of being so frustrated by what I don't see, I let God's Word be the lens through which I get to receive glimpses of His goodness that only those of us who suffer get to see?

Suffering can shrink our perspective. When we feel pain, we can become hyperfocused on fixing the source of the pain. We can think the only good move God could make is to take away the pain. And if that's all we are looking for, then we will become more frustrated and distrustful of God. (See more on this in this chapter's "One More Thing I Want You to Know" section.) But what if God's Word can help us see how to suffer and still be certain of His goodness?

Read the verses on the next page, and use this prompt to journal after each one:

When I read this verse, I see suffering isn't only this awful pain.

Suffering is also a way to _____

_____.

- "Not only so, but we also glory in our sufferings, because we know that suffering produces perseverance." (Romans 5:3)
- "When you pass through the waters, I will be with you; and when you pass through the rivers, they will not sweep over you. When you walk through the fire, you will not be burned; the flames will not set you ablaze." (Isaiah 43:2)
- "I remain confident of this: I will see the goodness of the LORD in the land of the living. Wait for the LORD; be strong and take heart and wait for the LORD." (Psalm 27:13–14)
- "The lowly he sets on high, and those who mourn are lifted to safety." (Job 5:11)
- "Very truly I tell you, you will weep and mourn while the world rejoices. You will grieve, but your grief will turn to joy." (John 16:20)

What if, instead of doubting God's goodness, I started cooperating with His goodness?

What does it mean to cooperate with God's goodness? It means to notice His goodness, to call it out, and to find calming enjoyment in those small evidences. Maybe we won't see the big miracle we keep looking for today. But we can see His goodness in other ways, right now, today.

This has become such a crucial aspect in my journey. When I don't see any good in a tough situation I'm going through, I think His goodness can only be evidenced by Him doing something to turn that situation around or at least something to assure me He's working on it. But I'm learning to expand my view and acknowledge His goodness in other places of my life. A lot of times I forget the small stuff is a direct result of our good Creator God. That's what helps me experience His goodness in very tangible ways. Here are some examples of small stuff that help me remember the big reality of God's goodness:

- the sweetness of a perfectly ripe peach
- music that calms my mind and makes me exhale
- the sun that comes out from behind a cloud and warms me on a chilly day
- lights that are strung between backyard trees, hanging above a circle of friends around a firepit
- an unexpected but truly satisfying belly laugh
- the smell of morning coffee, of my favorite flower, of my favorite dessert baking in the oven
- watching the ocean waves on a gorgeous day go just so far and then pull back inside themselves

Write down some of the evidence of the goodness of God you're experiencing in small, everyday ways. Then write down who you could share this with or give this to. When we spread His goodness to other people, we are cooperating with His goodness to us.

What if our suffering is what reveals God's goodness in the most intimate and personal ways?

Write down some ways you've personally experienced the goodness of God in the past.

- I felt God's goodness when He _____.
- Just the fact that I am _____ now is evidence of His goodness when I went through _____.
- I sometimes forget that _____ never would have happened in my life apart from the goodness of God.

What if I don't trust God? And what if I do?
Can I find a good outcome on my own? Would that outcome

come without challenges? Would that outcome require me to participate in the futile exercise of trying to change another person? To get
to that outcome, would I have to fix what I already know I can't fix
and control what I already know I can't control?

Do I really have the ability to find stability and safety and peace
and joy by going my own way? Is succumbing to the doubts and refusing to dig my roots deeper really going to help me better weather the
storms I'm facing?

Time for another deep breath. That's a whole lot to think through.

I'm going to end with us just sitting with those last questions.
Usually, I like my chapters to end with a big perspective change or
with solutions to our problems and answers to our questions. But this
isn't the chapter for that.

This is weighty stuff. Ultimately, trusting God is holding loosely
the parts of my life I want to hold most tightly. I want to trust Him,
until I don't. And that tension isn't one to solve. It's one to wrestle with
well in this temporary place called "now."

One More Thing I Want You to Know

I've really been sitting with this sentence I wrote: "Trusting
God is holding loosely the parts of my life I want to hold most
tightly." It is true. And God can be trusted. And God sometimes allows things to happen that bring deep sorrow. Can I
really simultaneously trust Him while soaking my pillow with
tears?

While I've certainly been hurt over the course of many
devastations, I haven't experienced all of the really painful things that can happen in life. So if reading this section
is too hard for you in your current situation, I give you full

permission to turn a page or two past this part. Maybe you'll return to it one day, and maybe you won't . . . and that's okay. Your journey with God and grief needs to be your own. But this is where I've landed.

Sorrow makes us hurt. Sorrow makes us grieve. Sorrow makes us feel out of control. Sorrow makes us feel anxious. Sorrow can sometimes feel like pouring gasoline on our doubts. Here's something I've been thinking through lately: we are to cast all of our anxiety on God, because He cares for us (1 Peter 5:7). Most of us have heard that verse but still find it hard to do when our pulse is racing, our heart is sinking, and our face is wet with tears.

If you keep reading 1 Peter 5, you'll see verse 7 is referring to the kind of anxiety associated with suffering. And the only instruction we are given before the command to cast our anxiety on Him is to humble ourselves:

> Humble yourselves, therefore, under God's mighty hand, that he may lift you up in due time. Cast all your anxiety on him because he cares for you.
>
> Be alert and of sober mind. Your enemy the devil prowls around like a roaring lion looking for someone to devour. Resist him, standing firm in the faith, because you know that the family of believers throughout the world is undergoing the same kind of sufferings.
>
> And the God of all grace, who called you to his eternal glory in Christ, after you have suffered a little while, will himself restore you and make you strong, firm and steadfast. (5:6–10)

My friend Meredith will often remind me of a challenge she received from the Lord: He can't lift an unbowed head. Whoa, what a powerful visual. When we keep looking at the outcomes we think are best and become fixated on the idea that our vision for our future is the only good one, our necks will become stiff from all that straining. But if we bow our heads in humility, we are in the right position for God to lift us up and point us in the direction He knows is best.

I guess this is part of what I've been missing.

Bowing instead of running.
Bowing instead of fixing.
Bowing instead of trying to make sense of stuff that
      may never make sense in our limited human
      minds.
Bowing instead of resisting Him.
Bowing instead of distrusting Him.
Bowing when things seem to be turning around.
Bowing when things fall apart again.
And bowing when the suffering makes us wonder about
      the goodness of God.

I've read these verses in 1 Peter many times, but I never tied this to my suffering. I never realized that suffering is actually a sign God is leading us in the exact right direction toward redemption. Suffering isn't a pitfall preventing our redemption. Suffering isn't proof that we should doubt God's goodness. Suffering doesn't mean that trusting God is too risky.

Suffering is our reminder to stay closer to God than ever before and not to resist His leading. God's way is the right way no matter how confusing it gets along the way. And God's time is the right time no matter how untimely it seems to us.

Remember:

- What my mind can't understand, my heart tends to distrust.
- Sometimes I can have more faith in my fears coming true than in God coming through for me.
- There will always be a gap between what we see and the full story God knows.
- If I don't feel like God is coming through for me today, it's so hard to trust that surrendering my future to Him is a safe thing to do.
- Suffering doesn't mean that trusting God is too risky.

Receive:

"Now faith is confidence in what we hope for and assurance about what we do not see." (Hebrews 11:1)

"I will instruct you and teach you in the way you
should go;
I will counsel you with my loving eye on
you." (Psalm 32:8)

"Your Father knows what you need before you ask him." (Matthew 6:8)

"When you pass through the waters,
        I will be with you;
and when you pass through the rivers,
        they will not sweep over you.
When you walk through the fire,
        you will not be burned;
        the flames will not set you ablaze."
                (Isaiah 43:2)

"I remain confident of this:
        I will see the goodness of the LORD
        in the land of the living.
Wait for the LORD;
        be strong and take heart
        and wait for the LORD." (Psalm 27:13–14)

Reflect:

- Identify some of the reasons you might resist trusting God enough to surrender the outcomes and your plans for how your life will go.
- Be honest with yourself: Do you see God as trustworthy? How has this chapter helped you better process this?
- What did the story of the ants and the tree reveal to you about "ants" in your own life?
- List some of the simple pleasures that serve as evidence of God's goodness to you. Which ones are your favorites?

Pray:

Father God,

I confess that I often attach my willingness to trust You to how my life is going at the moment. When things are going my way, it's easy to believe You are trustworthy. But when things fall apart, my trust in You wavers as I struggle to understand what You are doing. In the truth of my quiet moments and time in Your Word, I know You are good even when my life isn't. Today I choose to trust You with what I cannot see, do not know, do not want, and am afraid of. I surrender to You the outcomes and plans I have for the way my life should go.

In Jesus' name, amen.

Chapter Seven

How Can I Trust God When the Person Who Hurt Me Got Away with It?

•

It's so confusing when some of the people who do really wrong things seem to get away with what they did. It's especially hurtful when they claim God is for them and they are singing the same praise songs I am. They are claiming God is their good Father and asking Him to help them. But their seemingly faithful actions for everyone else to see do not line up with the way they treated me or someone I love.

And it can make me wonder, *Whose team is God on?* And then I feel bad even thinking that question, because I'm not perfect either. I do things I shouldn't. I disappoint people too.

But there always seem to be immediate consequences of my choices. So why does it feel like that's not what they face? Why does it look like their life is clicking right along with blessings even though I know they are not honoring God?

It's this kind of perceived unfairness that makes me feel like I'm slipping in my trust of God. I'm not losing faith in Him. I'm not questioning His unchanging truths. I don't have a life plan B where I walk away from Him. None of that. It's just that I want all the chaos to stop. And I want to know there will be just consequences for the sin that has taken place, so this person causing hurt will not keep unleashing hurt. And I know the only real way for this to happen is for God to intervene. But will He?

In the thick of the hurt and pain and shock of broken trust, the lack of tangible evidence that things will eventually be made right causes big questions to rattle about inside me. Is this world even set up in a way where there's motivation for people to be trustworthy? Or is it only set up for people to get what they want, no matter the hurt they cause others? Am I setting myself up for more pain when I trust people? If people seem to get away with what they do, then is everyone eventually going to be so self-preserving and self-serving that only fools dare to trust?

It can feel like if I'm a trusting, giving, and honest person, then I'm going to get hurt. But if I succumb to looking out only for myself and trusting no one, I'll live a very lonely existence.

Awesome. This is like one of those riddles I just can't solve. Maybe I'm a naive girl running through life like it's a field of daisies when it's really a field of land mines.

And that's when I pull out my journal and write, "Where are You, God? Where is the part of my story where You fix things, right wrongs, and bring good from all of this? Where is the payoff for doing the right things? Where are the consequences for those doing the wrong things? Come on, God. What are You doing?"

And, as a way to self-protect, I become self-reliant. I paint pictures in my mind of scenarios where my trust in God grows because things are finally turning out okay. There are ongoing hard circumstances that I wish I could finally write in my journal, "Look how God defended me. His justice finally came about. Look at how He brought it all together better than ever. This all makes sense now. I can finally exhale."

I don't have that page in my journal.

I have not seen the justice of God in several situations. Not yet. And maybe I won't on this side of eternity. I have really good parts of my life now. I am happy. But I still have to fight hard not to entertain the bitterness that invites me to pitch a tent right in the unfairness and camp out in it. Otherwise, constantly thinking about what God doesn't seem to be doing, and about my desire for my version of justice to come about, can become an unhealthy focus. This focus, over time, can become an obsession that, if left unattended, can become a stronghold for the enemy of my soul.

I think people assume all is well and my struggles are gone because, after so many years of heartbreak, I have a new man in my life who loves me and loves Jesus. But I still have to fight against the deep ache inside me that longs to see justice, not just for what happened in the death of my marriage but for what continues to happen.

Just a few months ago, out of the blue, a sheriff's deputy showed up at my door to deliver papers informing me I have to go to court and face my ex in another battle. Right when I thought I could start moving on, the past hurt became present hurt all over again.

I don't tell you this to solicit sympathy. I just want you to see that, however the unfairness of your situation is playing out, you're not alone. It's hard to fully step into the future when the past won't stay in the past. And it's doubly hard when my desire for things to be fair makes the fight against bitterness and resentment exhausting on a soul level. And it's triply (is that a word?) hard when it makes no sense why God isn't saying "no more" and stopping this.

I would imagine that, whether your trust and your heart have been broken by a friend, spouse, sibling, parent, leader, or another significant relationship, you understand the fight I'm talking about. If their hurtful actions are ongoing, I bet you're exhausted and frustrated too. Maybe, like me, parts of your story have turned around but someone is still causing pain.

Recently, a sweet gal who has experienced a journey a lot like mine sent me a message. She wanted me to know more about her story and how she thought she'd been obedient to God for the past decade after her divorce, but she was questioning that now because she was still alone and her life was still really difficult. She wanted to know if I would be so positive and confident in trusting the Lord if I wasn't experiencing a new relationship.

Such a fair and understandable question. Trusting God without seeing the redemption we thought we'd get to see by now can feel like the deepest betrayal of all. It's also what builds our faith, but sometimes we'd rather have relief than another learning opportunity.

I sat with her question for a good long while. I don't hang out in my DMs often and rarely get to respond as much as I would like to. But since I happened to read this message, I knew I needed to respond. And I didn't want my answer to just gloss over her deep pain with a few cliché sentences and a Bible verse. She deserved more than that.

And so do you.

This is what I wrote back:

I've spent many nights staring up into the sky, bewildered as I felt my disappointment turn into grief turn into numbness turn into distancing from God. There were so many times when I thought God was about to turn everything around, but then things got worse, not better. Some of my darkest days were when I could not make sense of what God was allowing. And my fear was that because God allowed all of this, what else might He allow?

Slowly, I have realized I cannot attach my hope to God making things feel fair. And I certainly can't attach my hope to the outcomes I desperately want. I have to attach my hope to who God is. He is good. He is faithful. He is my Father who loves me.

God's character, which never changes, is His personal promise to me. And to you. We can stand with assurance on who He is even when we don't understand what He does or doesn't do. There are still hurtful things happening surrounding my divorce too. I wish this wasn't the case for either of us.

I am grateful God has brought a man who loves Jesus into my life and all the joy that comes along with being in a healthy relationship. But even this gift comes with its own fears and uncertainties. So, my challenge now is not to tie my hope of a better future to this new man. It's the same lesson I was learning during the many years of feeling so very alone. It's the same lesson once again, just with different challenges.

I've asked the same question when my friends found new love while I was still in the midst of intense loneliness. It's so hard. I understand and so wish I could look into your future and whisper back to you all the wonderful things ahead of you. While I can't do that, I can promise God is at work. Hang on, beautiful friend.

I wanted to make more concrete promises to her about what God is working on. I would have loved to give her a time frame to help ease her angst. I would love for there to be a way to make this possible for all of us. But if it was good for us to have this information, God would surely give it to us. So, the fact that He isn't allowing us access to these specific details lets me know that having that information isn't what's best.

Charles Spurgeon preached a sermon that applies to this very struggle. It is a little heady, but the wisdom contained within his words is worth thinking about.

Every affliction is timed and measured, and every comfort is sent with a loving thoughtfulness which makes it precious in a sevenfold degree. O believer, the great thoughtfulness of the divine mind is exercised towards you, the chosen of the Lord. Never has anything happened to you as the result of a remorseless fate; but all your circumstances have been ordered in wisdom by a living, thoughtful, loving Lord.

. . . Our heavenly Father knows what he is doing; when his ways towards us appear to be involved and complicated, and we cannot disentangle the threads of the skein, yet the Lord sees all things clearly, and knows the thoughts that he thinks towards us. He never misses his way, nor becomes embarrassed. We dare not profess to understand the ways of God to man: they are past finding out. Providence is a great deep. Its breadth exceeds the range of our vision, and its depth baffles our profoundest thought.[14]

My favorite lines are "Our heavenly Father knows what he is doing; when his ways towards us appear to be involved and complicated, and we cannot disentangle the threads of the skein, yet the Lord sees all things clearly." Yes, He does. And I do not see all things clearly. So I haven't figured it all out, but I do have some hard-earned wisdom that will be good to think through together. Working through what we don't understand—especially when asking, *How can I trust God when the person who hurt me got away with it?*—will not be a tidy answer to all our questions. But we can manage the tension better if we are equipped with truth.

Just because these doubts are where our thoughts are today doesn't mean this is where our thoughts should stay. We must keep fighting to make sure our first words filled with anguish aren't our last words filled with bitterness. And the best way to fight through our toughest questions about God's justice is to create space in our thoughts for more of God's perspective.

If you get nothing else out of this chapter, I want you to get this: we may never see the justice we long for on this side of eternity. Some will. But many will not. I can't explain this, but I'm working hard to accept this.

Some days I feel like I can make peace with this.

Other days I try, but it's so hard. Really, really hard.

But I'm learning that doing something else besides obsessing over my doubts and questions is necessary. And by "doing something else," I don't mean escaping. Sometimes, I have this slight

We must keep fighting to make sure our first words filled with anguish aren't our last words filled with bitterness.

desire to just run away from my life. I have often said, "I think I'll just go to Montana and become a waitress. Or a private investigator. Or a poetry writer using a pseudonym. I'll live in a remote cabin with squirrels and racoons as my only companions."

Hello, Lysa. Reality is calling . . . please answer.

Okay, so none of those are realistic solutions for today. So I stop searching for cabins to rent and instead call someone wise who can bring me back to reality. When my mind is stuck on a loop of asking questions I already know there aren't answers for right now, it helps to reach out to a friend who knows how to process struggles while factoring in biblical wisdom. I don't need a friend to jump in and tell me that what I've been through justifies retaliation. I need a friend who will say this is really hard and acknowledge the depth of unfairness that seems to be at play here. But then I need her to remind me that the absence of justice isn't evidence of the absence of God. I want her to acknowledge my struggle but not jump into my spiraling thoughts with me. Oh, and if she's there in person and brings a slice of chocolate cake with her, that's good too. Her presence helps me feel God's presence.

But there are other times when I just can't talk about my struggles. It's like I'm so pulled into the pain, the words can't find their way out of me. And I'm too exhausted to process with a friend. On those days, I know it's crucial for me to take my shoes off and

The absence of *justice* isn't evidence of the absence of God.

get outside. My counselor once suggested this, and, as much as I doubted him, it really does help to stand on solid ground and see that the sky is not falling.

When I'm wondering where God is, His creation always seems to have a message about Him, if I pay close enough attention. A verse I love to quote is Psalm 19:1: "The heavens declare the glory of God; the skies proclaim the work of his hands." If I can't see the work of His hands the way I thought I would in my circumstances, I want to see His work somewhere.

One afternoon, I was sitting on the shore, trying to stop my desire to book a ticket to Montana for real this time. Earlier that morning I had received an email informing me a harsh article had just been released, detailing why I was being taken to court. The lawsuit had already caused me so much anxiety and pain. The accusations were troubling, and I had plenty of evidence to refute them.

The person writing the article about me never contacted me to check the facts. So they took the allegations from the lawsuit and published them for all the world to read. Other media outlets followed suit. And there was nothing I could do about it. But you know what hurt most of all? These were all Christian media outlets. And the person suing me claimed to have a team of people praying for them. Whether this was true, I don't know. But the thought that people who knew about the history of heartbreak and deception were now praying against me and my children . . . it was not just confusing, it was maddening.

If you can't count on Christians to be on the side of truth, then who can you trust?

I was having a hard time getting my pulse to slow down and my hands to stop shaking. I just kept staring out at this big, vast ocean, asking God, *Why? Why does it seem like, once again, a person who already caused me so much pain is getting away with it?* I don't know how long I sat there in stunned silence. But eventually I noticed the salty water was inching closer and closer. The tide was coming in, and I knew if I didn't move, the water would soon wash over me and my stuff.

Part of me thought, *Fine, wash it all out to sea.* But another thought came to me: *The beauty of the ocean comes with the reality of the tide.*

I started repeating this sentence over and over until there was more to it.

Many things in life come as a package deal. When we choose to participate with part of it, we participate with all of it. Relationships are this way. Jobs are this way. Owning a home is this way. Even vacations are this way. All these things are package deals—they come with enticing parts and challenging parts. And sin is no different. When someone commits some kind of sin against you, whatever seems so enticing about the sin will always come with the consequences of that sin.

When other people intentionally wrong us and blatantly hurt us but never seem to suffer consequences for any of it, this apparent lack of fairness is what can resurrect the bitterness we thought we'd dealt with, and it can certainly increase distrust.

It took time for me to keep thinking through this. But eventually I recognized the truth that helped me and still helps me manage the unfairness of hurtful situations: when people sin against us, they unleash into their lives the consequences of that sin. We may never see it. In fact, it may look like they just got away with everything. But today we can be reminded that eventually "they will eat the fruit of their ways and be filled with the fruit of their schemes" (Proverbs 1:31).

The best thing we can do is trust God with their consequences while making sure we don't get lured into sinful choices trying to right the wrongs.

I know God has comfort and instruction in His Word if only I will open it up . . . but I also have to be willing to open my heart and mind so I can receive it.

Ironically, during this same week the articles about me were released, I was reviewing some devotions I'd written in the past. One was on the story of Esther, and it hit me in such a different way this time around.

For most of the book of Esther, it appears a man named Haman, who wanted to kill the Jewish people, was going to get away with his devious plan. God seemingly wasn't intervening. Evil looked like it was going to win. But eventually things begin to change, and we arrive in Esther 7 to read the account of Haman's downfall, ultimately leading to his death.

Haman's pride backfired, and his evil intentions led to his own humiliation. Haman, the one who had been scheming to kill others, became the one begging for his own life (7:7). The very gallows he'd built to kill Esther's beloved relative and guardian, Mordecai, became the place of his own death (v. 10). He ate the fruit of his own wicked schemes.

Now, let's pause before we start fist-bumping and saying, "Yeah, they got what was coming to them." Trust me—I'm tempted to celebrate when those who have caused destruction and devastation experience hardships I think they deserve. But I need to remember that adding more hate and hurt never healed anyone, and it isn't wise. It certainly wouldn't help me find peace. James 3:13–18 teaches us there is wisdom that comes down from above, but there is also another kind of earthly "wisdom" that can be unspiritual and demonic.

> Who is wise and understanding among you? By his good conduct let him show his works in the meekness of wisdom. But if you have bitter jealousy and selfish ambition in your hearts, do not boast and be false to the truth. This is not the wisdom that comes down from above, but is earthly, unspiritual, demonic. For where jealousy and selfish ambition exist, there will be disorder and every vile practice. But the wisdom from above is first pure, then peaceable, gentle, open to reason, full of mercy and good fruits, impartial and

sincere. And a harvest of righteousness is sown in peace by those who make peace. (ESV)

I'm going to set aside what, in my flesh, I think they deserve and remember we are called to pray for our enemies so God can lead them to repentance. And that doesn't mean we pray for them to suffer. After all, we always want God's mercy to be in play, because we need it too. We need to remember that sinning against others isn't just what those people who hurt us did. You and I are sinners too. We have hurt and will hurt others. We have sinned and will again sin against others. Sin blinds us all.

Haman's sin blinded him, made him hard-hearted, and eventually caught up with him because that's what sin always does. Many times throughout Scripture, when sin is mentioned, it's coupled with being unaware or blinded by our own desires or a hardening of the heart. Hebrews 3:12–13 reminds us of this: "See to it, brothers and sisters, that none of you has a sinful, unbelieving heart that turns away from the living God. But encourage one another daily, as long as it is called 'Today,' so that none of you may be hardened by sin's deceitfulness."

In whatever we are facing, we don't want to do wrong things to try to bring about right things. We can commit to keep our hearts pure and place our trust in the safest place—with God. He doesn't leave sin unaddressed: "It is mine to avenge; I will repay. In due time their foot will slip; their day of disaster is near and their doom rushes upon them" (Deuteronomy 32:35). He sees all. And He is always present.

In the book of Esther, where God's name is not even mentioned, His presence is very much still there. No human could have possibly arranged what happened. But sometimes God moves in incredible ways without calling any attention to Himself at all. Esther certainly did her part, as did many others. But, once again, they didn't do wrong things to try to bring about the right things. Doing things God's way and in God's timing is the right way and the right timing.

This isn't the only time in Scripture where an evil plan looked like it was going to win. In the life of Jesus, His enemies—King Herod, the Pharisees and Sadducees, and Pontius Pilate, to name a few—believed they had created a foolproof plan to get rid of the Messiah and to overthrow His reign. But the men who came against Jesus were not the only villains in the story. The ultimate villain was the Enemy, Satan, and other malevolent evil forces that he leads. The irony is that the very plan of Satan led to the redemptive story of Jesus. The Enemy set Jesus on the journey to the cross, but with every step Jesus took, the Enemy drew closer to defeat. In a similar reversal, the agenda and strategy of Haman was used against him to bring about his own demise.

In both stories:

- There was an evil plan.
- There was an enemy.
- People were going to be destroyed if someone didn't step in to save them.
- A hero came from humble beginnings and looked nothing like what the people expected.
- The heroes remained humble and honored God in their approach to handling the dire situation.
- The heroes were uniquely positioned by God to fulfill the plan of God.
- The heroes set aside what was best for them for a greater purpose.[15]

In the case of Haman's death, the guilty died in place of the innocent. In the case of Jesus, the innocent died in place of the guilty.

Oh, friend, I pray we cling to this truth today: darkness, sin, and hopelessness have been overcome. Jesus did it for me. And He did it for you. Jesus loves you. Jesus sees you. The battle you're facing, no matter how dark it feels, isn't hopeless. We may not be able to see victory right now, but because of Jesus, evil is in the process of being ultimately defeated. The world as we know it now, plagued with sin and pain, is not our home. The new heaven and the new earth are much closer than we think (Revelation 21:3–8). But for now, our assignment is to keep following God and keep trusting Him.

I know it's not easy, especially when so much of what we are facing feels incredibly unfair.

Sometimes I think I hold on to the burden of unfairness because I don't see tangible evidence of God doing anything. But this is what I'm reminding myself of: we don't serve a do-nothing God. Even in the silence, the unknown, and the places where it looks like evil is winning, He is working. We may experience evil in this world, but even still, God reigns over evil. There is a Savior of the world who will right all the wrongs. Even if it takes a really long time and even if I don't see it in my lifetime. Victorious Jesus will have victory in the wrongs done to you and the evil committed against you. This doesn't mean I give up. It means I'm giving over to God what was never mine to carry.

And in the meantime, we simply have to leave room for the mystery of God. Romans 11:33–36 (CSB) reminds us of this:

> Oh, the depth of the riches
> and the wisdom and the knowledge of God!
> How unsearchable his judgments
> and untraceable his ways!
> For who has known the mind of the Lord?
> Or who has been his counselor?
> And who has ever given to God,
> that he should be repaid?
> For from him and through him
> and to him are all things.
> To him be the glory forever. Amen.

One More Thing I Want You to Know

I have a friend named Jenny who has suffered through a lot of unfair circumstances. She decided to join a support group with others who have similar circumstances. At their meetings they give updates on what's happening with their lives. Each week she hears about the struggles and victories of the women in her group. Of course, she celebrates with every person who experiences their prayers being answered. Jenny is very mature in her faith, and she's one of the most gracious people I know. But sometimes it's hard to hear about God answering other people's prayers while she's still waking up to confusion and heartbreaking realities every day.

As she prayed about this and wrestled through it, one day she had an epiphany. She spoke a sentence out loud that brought a lot of comfort to her heart. When she told me about how she now better manages other people's celebrations while she's still hurting, I knew it was a game changer for my perspective as well. Jenny said, "Their path to see God's glory is different from mine."

We are all on a journey. God is with us. God is for us. But how He leads us and where He leads us will always be a bit of a mystery. But what doesn't have to be mysterious is this: we will see God's glory either on this side of eternity or on the other side. His glory will not be mocked. His glory will not be denied. His glory will be seen by those who have given their hearts to Him. We just might travel different paths than others around us.

Wow. I pray this helps you as much as it has helped me.

Remember:

- It's hard to fully step into the future when the past won't stay in the past.
- We must keep fighting to make sure our first words filled with anguish aren't our last words filled with bitterness.
- I cannot attach my hope to God making things feel fair. And I certainly can't attach my hope to the outcomes I desperately want. I have to attach my hope to who God is.
- The absence of justice isn't evidence of the absence of God.
- Doing things God's way and in God's timing is the right way and the right timing.

Receive:

"They will eat the fruit of their ways
and be filled with the fruit of their
schemes." (Proverbs 1:31)

"Who is wise and understanding among you? By his good conduct let him show his works in the meekness of wisdom. But if you have bitter jealousy and selfish ambition in your hearts, do not boast and be false to the truth. This is not the wisdom that comes down from above, but is earthly, unspiritual, demonic. For where jealousy and selfish ambition exist, there will be disorder and every vile practice. But the wisdom from above is first pure, then peaceable, gentle, open to reason, full of mercy and good fruits, impartial and sincere. And a harvest of righteousness is sown in peace by those who make peace." (James 3:13–18 ESV)

Reflect:

- How do you relate to this statement: "God seems to be making things right for other people but not for me in the situation I'm facing"? What helps you manage that feeling of unfairness?
- What fresh perspectives do you need to keep in mind when it seems like the ones who hurt you got away with it?

Pray:

Heavenly Father,

Even when I'm faced with what feels unfair in my life and relationships, I know I can count on Your character never changing. Your justice and mercy bring me comfort. Thank You for overcoming the darkness, sin, and hopelessness I see all around me. You are working and will right all wrongs. Help me give over to You all the things that were never mine to carry.

In Jesus' name, amen.

Chapter Eight

What We Don't Trust, We Will Try to Control

•

I was talking to a friend the other day about defining *life* in one sentence. We decided the sentence should be: "Life . . . it's not what I expected." Life sometimes works like a surprise party. Other times like a surprise attack. The only thing certain is that it will be filled with the unexpected.

I know this, but I still have this driving sense inside me that if I just know enough, worry enough, research enough, plan enough, arrange enough, talk things through enough, stay ahead of things enough, and make sure everyone else is on the same page as me, then I can keep life going like it should go. My expectations of how life should play out are for the good of all my people. For me, the more my life deviates from my definition of *good*, the more I want to try to control the uncontrollable. It's not that this is all bad. After all, I want to be responsible. But I need to check myself to make sure my desire to be responsible doesn't cross over into the impossible task of controlling the uncontrollable.

It's odd how sneaky this desire to control is. After all, I've never really considered myself a controlling person. For the most part, I am easygoing and flexible, and I like other people to make the plans so I can just go along with the group.

When I think of someone who is controlling, I usually think of people engaging in the more overt and emotionally abusive tactics like threatening, isolating, blaming, humiliating, acting possessive, obsessively monitoring someone to extreme degrees, and taking away someone's ability to choose for themselves. That's not the type of control I'm talking about in this chapter. The type of control I'm referencing here is my desire to keep myself and those I love from experiencing hardships and heartbreaks.

That doesn't sound so bad, right? Don't we all want to prevent bad things from happening as much as we can? Yes, but where I can slip into unhealthy patterns is through trying to prevent what is beyond my ability to control. After all, if I can prevent bad things from happening, then I don't have to rely on or trust anyone else. I don't have to participate in that terrifying unknown of people making choices that mess everything up or put everything at risk. And I don't have to participate in that sometimes terrifying unknown of trusting God, who allows things that are so very confusing at best and devastating at worst.

But my desire to control—it's an illusion. Or possibly a delusion. It's presumptuous of me and prideful to think I know what's best. And yet the most tender places of my heart, the ones that shake with fear because I can't stand the thought of another awful thing being added to my family's story, keep saying, "Please try. Because maybe this time you can hold it all together."

Trust can feel like betraying my best efforts to keep it all together while others aren't paying nearly enough attention to things.

Sigh.

I want my relationships to be bulletproof. I want everyone I love to have the same ideas as I do about what is best. I want to control the narrative so others don't see me in a bad light or so I don't look underqualified, dumb, or like I don't have my stuff together. I want to construct safety nets around anything that feels risky to me. I want God to be predictable. And I want life to be safe, feel good, and go according to plan.

Maybe that's your desire as well. Or maybe your desires for control play out differently. One of my friends said, for her, control looks like always cleaning up after her family rather than being able to sit with them and enjoy time together. It's not just about her being responsible. It's crossed over into being obsessive about the cleanliness.

She can also recognize it when she's checking and rechecking her kids' backpacks every night before bed. Her kids are at an age where they are capable of getting their stuff together themselves. But, if she lets them do it, she risks the next morning being chaotic if they forget something. She doesn't want to risk being late for work because she has to turn around and go back for something they forgot. Or, worse yet, she doesn't want the school to call her in the middle of the day, telling her she needs to bring the missing item to school. That's understandable, right? As we continued talking about it, the real issue turned out to be that she doesn't want her kids to suffer by not having what they need like she constantly did as a child. Bottom line, she doesn't want to be like her mother. She doesn't just want to help her kids. She wants to prevent them from suffering the consequences of their sometimes irresponsible choices. And she doesn't want to look like a mom who can't keep things together. Again, she doesn't want the teachers to perceive her to be irresponsible in extreme ways like her mother was.

However control plays out for you and whatever reasons there are that shaped you this way, please know that trying to keep things under control using realistic measures is a good quality. But if you and I are holding on so tightly that our stress levels and anxiety are making it challenging for others to be around us, or we are constantly on edge with burnout nipping at our emotions, we need to recognize this isn't a sustainable way to live. In other words, if we clench our jaws throughout our days, it will be really hard to smile about and enjoy our lives.

Where does this anxiety come from? For me, it's the tension between what I want and what is actually happening. When something doesn't feel right, look right, or go according to plan, I want to do whatever I can to fix it. I can't stand to get caught off guard. If something bad is going to happen, I at least want to see it coming in time to brace for impact. I want to manage the fallout before it happens. I want to manage my reputation as a mom, friend, daughter, sister, ministry worker, and leader. Surely all my efforts will guarantee there will be so much less suffering for me and those I do life with.

As a result, I do mental gymnastics trying to control the play. *If I do this, then of course she will do that, right? I better not say no, because if I do, it will just push her further away. I bet if I give this, then she will get back on track. If I promise this, then she will stop making that mistake. If we just do x, y, and z, then things will go so much better for all of us. If I can just gather enough proof to show them my perspective, then they will want to do what I'm suggesting. Surely he will see the same red flags I do if I help him become aware of his blind spots. Life will work like it should if we are all cautious, careful, and courteous and we all count the cost before we make decisions. Okay?*

Sometimes, when people I do life with make unexpected choices and hard circumstances ensue, I feel like I'm standing on the edge of a cliff with people who are bound and determined to go in a direction opposite of my definition of right, fair, and good. Some are teetering on the edge of the cliff. They don't plan to jump, but they are stressing me out with their risky decisions. Others are in full-blown jump mode. They are acting like it's no big deal—as if the drop is only a few feet. Meanwhile, I see an impending doom that they are oblivious to. I'm baffled that they don't see the danger. I'm freaked out by their carelessness.

I run from one person to the next, pulling them back. But as quickly as I get them away from the edge, they just keep returning. I can't stand the thought of them going over the edge. I know these people. I love these people. Each of them carries a piece of my heart with them. When they hurt, I hurt. Their choices affect not only their lives but mine as well.

I desperately want them to return to a place of safety. For me, a crucial part of trusting someone is knowing I can count on them to act responsibly and to put the same level of consideration into their choices as I put into mine. I want them to play their choices out and see the same potentially awful outcomes that I do.

It's not that I want them to think exactly like I do—I realize we are all different. And that's a good thing, because I might be wrong in my assessment. But I'm going to have a difficult time believing it's safe to trust their assessment if they don't have a good track record of making wise choices. If I start to sniff out that they aren't really thinking things through, I feel compelled to get involved.

Because if they are throwing caution to the wind, I know there's a high likelihood I'll be the one they turn to if things fall apart. And I'm afraid of the consequences we'll both suffer if things turn out poorly. I'm exhausted by picking up the pieces of things I didn't shatter.

Sigh again. My brain is so tired from always trying to be one step ahead of the great unraveling I fear will happen if I don't step in. What about you? How do you see controlling tendencies sneaking into your life? I surveyed some of my friends about this, and here is the list that emerged:

- needing to know every detail
- obsessively trying to figure out how to prevent bad things from happening

- going to unusual lengths to ensure you're not caught off guard
- getting annoyed when people deviate from your plan
- having unrealistic expectations of others
- assuming others are incapable
- overplanning
- being overly rigid with boundaries
- thinking your way is the best way
- resorting to guilt-tripping
- using the silent treatment
- having a bad attitude when asked to be flexible
- treating small annoyances as epic offenses
- looking for opportunities to say, "I told you so"
- refusing to let others see your vulnerable side so you can stay in charge
- recruiting others to put pressure on the one you feel isn't cooperating with your plan

If you see some of your own tendencies listed here, please know that this list isn't meant to shame you. This isn't just my issue or your issue; it's a human issue. Some things in the list stem from good intentions and are in keeping with the way God has wired you (being detail oriented, for example). When they are planted in the right soil, these are great qualities. But note we're talking about taking these qualities to an extreme, to a place where they're used to control.

This list gives us a starting place to consider where the chaos of controlling might be stealing our peace. All these things on the list are understandable in some circumstances. But when they are the go-to patterns for how we cope with relational risk and fear of the unknown, we need to work on this.

Remember: controlling others isn't going to bring about the life we want. The illusion of control makes big promises but will never deliver. It won't make us safer. It won't prevent heartbreak from happening. It won't make life less complicated. It won't bring about what we are desperate for. And it won't make our relationships stable enough for real trust to grow.

If we think we are the stabilizing force keeping everything together and everyone else in line, we will be exhausted and disillusioned by people's imperfections. And we will fret and worry and possibly even have panic attacks when we see much safer routes in life but the people we love refuse to take them.

Even if we have good intentions with our efforts to control, and even if we are absolutely correct that if we don't hold things together, they will fall apart, our human efforts aren't sustainable. We may be able to patch a few things together for a short time, but we can't fix what is beyond our ability to fix.

I know this. But I sure don't live like I know it when I allow my desire for control to sneak back in time and time again.

As I look at that list of indicators of control, for me, not wanting to get caught off guard is a really big one. I don't want to be unprepared. That makes me feel that I look irresponsible and oblivious to things I should have been aware of. I don't want situations to hit me before I've braced for impact.

I think many of us are like that, right? Maybe you don't want to get caught off guard because you don't want to be embarrassed. You don't want others to have something they can use against you. You don't want to be wrongly judged as incapable. You don't want to look foolish. Or maybe you don't like feeling as though you got left in the dark when others know something you aren't aware of.

All this control stuff is hard to admit and process, so let me add in a little levity here. Sister, what I am about to share is a true story, and it can be verified by all ten thousand souls who were present that unfortunate day. To a girl who doesn't like getting caught off guard, this one was a doozy.

It was one of the first times I got asked to speak at an arena event this large. I was incredibly nervous. Like, knee-knocking, hand-shaking, mouth-as-dry-as-a-cotton-ball nervous. At this particular event, there were sponsors, and the speakers were supposed to do appeals to support the sponsors in addition to giving their message. Since I do not have the spiritual gift of announcements, I asked the coordinators to write down every detail of the sponsor announcement I was supposed to make. Luckily, they told me I wouldn't have to say a word because two other speakers would be doing all the talking. All I had to do was hand out child-sponsorship packets. *Great,* I thought.

This child-sponsorship organization was one that does amazing work to help impoverished children around the world have food, water, and learning opportunities while teaching them about Jesus. I have a child I sponsor through a different organization with a similar mission, but I wasn't familiar with the details of how this sponsorship program worked. So just handing out the packets seemed like the best job for me. I verified with those in charge several times that I absolutely wouldn't have to say anything.

When the other two speakers and I took the stage to invite the crowd to participate in this worthy cause, I had a tote bag full of sponsor packets. I was ready to hand them out to anyone who raised their hand. So, there I was, just standing up on the stage, smiling and feeling confident about the job I had been assigned. But what happened next was, well, a disaster. It really was.

The other two speakers got moved in some way and felt compelled to grab my tote bag and hand me the microphone. Then they went off into the crowd that was now staring at me, waiting for me to give all the details. The details that were on the cards the speakers were carrying far, far away from me.

The arena was silent. The spotlight on me was very bright. And my mind was very blank.

I knew zero details. And with every painfully quiet second that ticked by, the atmosphere of that arena was getting more and more awkward. I tried to swallow hard, but there wasn't a drop of saliva to make this possible. I had to say something. But what?!

I decided that instead of making up the details and really messing things up for everybody, I would just find a way to relate to the struggles of these children in need of sponsors. Surely if I talked for a bit, the other speakers would come back with those announcement cards!

With wide eyes and a heart thumping out of my chest, I opened my mouth. What I intended to say was, "I relate to being a child in a situation that feels hopeless." Instead, what came out of my mouth was, "I, too, used to be one of these children."

The entire audience gasped. And suddenly it dawned on me that they thought I used to be a child in this sponsorship program. I tried to clarify, but there was no fixing this. I was now knee-deep in a testimony that wasn't mine. The more I talked, the worse the unintentional, panicked lie got.

It was so bad the producer of the event walked in front of the stage and mouthed, *"Stop! Stop! Stop! Stop! Stop!"* If they had a trapdoor, I feel certain they would have opened it and let the stage swallow me whole. The good news is many children were sponsored that day. The bad news is I never figured out how to correct this—until now.

You better believe I will never walk on a stage and make any kind of announcement unless I have every detail written out on a card that I carry in my very own hands.

This experience of getting caught off guard is now a funny story. But with other times when I've been caught off guard in hurtful ways, I have to fight really hard to keep my heart soft and open. I want to put my fists up and get defensive. Or I want to bow out, crawl into my bed, and will the world to leave me alone.

But the Lord wants me to bow down and realize nothing catches Him off guard.

Humans who break our trust do not have the power to break

apart God's good plans for our lives. They may have enough influence in our lives to hurt our hearts and make us feel derailed. We may even think their actions have created so much destruction that life will never be normal again. But people are never more powerful than God.

While there will always be gaps in the trust we have with people, there are no gaps in the trustworthiness of God.

That's not meant to be a quick little "Christianese" Band-Aid we slap onto situations when we don't know what else to say. It's a statement of hard-earned truth that I'm going to need you to remind me of the next time you find me riddled with anxiety because someone I love is going in a direction that is seriously freaking me out. And it's a truth I want us to hold on to as we read the rest of this chapter. People are never more powerful than God.

Humans who break our trust do not have the power to break apart God's good plans for our lives.

His Word assures us of this over and over with truths like Lamentations 3:22–23: "The steadfast love of the LORD never ceases; his mercies never come to an end; they are new every morning; great is your faithfulness" (ESV). Not only do these verses assure us with strong and definitive statements like "never ceases," "never come to an end," and "great is your faithfulness," but I love the phrase "new every morning." Think of how confident you are when something is new. When something is old, it can start to wear out and become less and less dependable. God's mercies never wear out, and they never become less and less dependable.

But if we are going to receive the benefit of this assurance, we have to believe it, hold on to it, and speak it out loud when the doubts come. And they will come.

After I had my trust broken in harsh and unexpected ways, trying to control became a survival skill. During the years when I was constantly caught off guard and life spun out of control, I lost a lot of my laid-back nature. I remember how text messages or phone calls from certain people during that season made me hold my breath and brace for impact. There was just so much bad news coming at me that I felt compelled to try to control each of the sources of chaos.

In the end it didn't work. Trying to control and manage situations and people left me with patterns of thought, doubts, and triggers I am still trying to undo. I am having to retrain my thinking that a different plan doesn't mean a bad plan. It's scary but necessary to practice overcoming my fear of the unexpected by letting things in my life unfold differently than I thought they would.

I've made some real progress with this. But I still struggle at times with the people closest to me. The closer I am to someone and the more their choices have a direct effect on me, the more anxious I feel when they do something I didn't see coming.

Can you relate?

The things we don't understand about someone will likely be the things we don't trust in them. And that which we don't trust, we'll try to control.

Like I said, sometimes I try to take control by getting intense, more direct, and hyperfocused on fixing the situation at hand. Other times I'll do the opposite extreme and just bow out, shut down, withdraw, and avoid. But those actions are also a form of control.

Now, can I just state something for both of us? Of course we do this. Some people in our lives have disappointed us, proven they don't have our best interests in mind, seriously messed up, lied to us, hidden things from us, made us feel powerless, made us look foolish, and told us things were fine when they weren't fine at all. We paid a high price for their actions. When people have a bad track record, of course it's not wise to keep blindly trusting them. But we also don't want to make our future relationships pay for the sins of the people who broke our trust in the past.

That's the biggest of all risks in this journey. It's not that we will risk trusting and possibly have our hearts broken again. It's that we won't grow and heal from what happened. As long as we are paralyzed in the vicious cycle of trying to control people or avoid people, we will attract that same level of dysfunction in future relationships. We won't move on toward the healthy, trusting relationships we want. We will stay stuck right in that same pit of pain where we are angry at the people who betrayed us, trying to control what we don't trust, doubting that God really has good in store for us, and limiting the possibilities for our future.

What a sad thing it would be if our only definition of moving forward was inviting other unhealed people into our pit of pain. That's where I was for a while. But it's not where I am now. And I suspect, because you are reading this book, it's not where you are either. I am so proud of you and thankful that God brought us together in these pages so we can keep growing alongside each other.

One of the main things we need to heal from is believing the only way to self-protect is to keep a sense of control over others and circumstances. When we are being controlling, we think it's the quickest way to reestablish safety, eliminate stress, and prevent what we are afraid will happen. However, it's actually doing the opposite. Because when we take over, we are basically telling God to move over and let us take it from here.

Recently I had the opportunity to visit the command center aboard an extremely large ship. Toward the end of the tour, the captain asked if I would like to sit in his seat. As I sat down, I couldn't help but be amazed at all the skill and expertise necessary to safely run this vessel.

My friends who were with me took several pictures of me looking like I was in control. But it was an illusion. I didn't have the knowledge or the experience to do anything helpful unless the captain instructed me. Can you imagine what a foolish request it would have been if I'd asked the captain, who was fully capable and fully equipped, to entrust his ship into my fully incapable hands? I can verify, without hesitation, that me being in control of that ship would have been a risk no one wanted to take. It may have felt good to feel in control for a few minutes, but if I wanted to return home safely, I had to turn the control over to the captain.

Just as in life, there are dangers in the sea that only the captain knows how to handle.

Trying to carry the weight of holding everything and everybody together is a role God never called us to carry. And it's taking a great toll on our peace.

I have learned the hard way that trying to control people won't pave the way to building healthy trust with people. And even more important, I've also had to learn I'm not always right. Sometimes I see a cliff of impending doom that's really just a curbside step.

Now, I want to slow down for a minute and acknowledge how tough it is to release some of the ways we control, because honestly our motivation isn't that we always want to be in charge but rather that we want to be safe. Sometimes I catch myself mentally running into the future where I fear there is impending doom and then trying to make wise choices today to steer away from trouble as much as I can. Sometimes this is wise. But while it's good to plan for the future, we don't want to obsess over the future. We can control our choices today, but we cannot fully control the outcomes of tomorrow. I don't like that last sentence any more than you do.

With this whole trust journey, I'm having to learn how to acknowledge what may or may not happen in the future but make the choice to live in today. This is what I can control: making wise choices right now, knowing God is in full control. This is what I can't control: all that happens in the tomorrows to come. In Matthew 6:34 Jesus reminds us, "Therefore do not worry about tomorrow, for tomorrow will worry about itself. Each day has enough trouble of its own." So hard to live out sometimes but so very good to keep in mind always.

I'm also learning how to trust and who to trust while at the same time balancing my expectations of people. Trying to keep everything and everyone in line with our expectations is an impossible task that ultimately makes us more anxious, not less. If my end goal is never to get caught off guard again, I'll set myself up for failure. I have to acknowledge I will have my trust broken again in small ways and big ways. It's impossible to control people and circumstances in such a way that I don't ever get hurt again. And certainly my goal with trusting God can't be to reduce Him down to being predictable. Instead, my goal should be to continuously do my best to place my trust in God and carefully and reasonably place responsible conditions on trusting others.

Sometimes I will give trust to those I shouldn't. And sometimes I will withhold trust from people when I shouldn't. I won't ever get it all right. And I won't get it all wrong. But I will suffer much more in the process when I pull away from God and try to take control of it all myself.

The more I try to force the life I want, the less likely I am to get it. The more I try to force the relationships I want, the less likely I am to enjoy the people in front of me. The more I demand an unrealistic perfection from others, the less my relationships will go the distance. The more I refuse to trust God when He says no, the more I'll miss that this might be His protection over me. The more I get impatient with God's timetable, the more I'll walk right by the beauty God has for me today. With a sullen look and a heavy heart, I could miss it all.

Now, I want us both to take a deep breath as we ponder the question: What do we do about it?

We sit in this moment and make the choice to receive our life today just as it is. I would imagine that you, like me, have lifted up many prayers to God about what you are desperate for Him to do with all you're facing right now. And I believe with all my heart that today is part of the answer to those many prayers.

This is what I can control: making wise choices *right now*, knowing God is in *full control*. This is what I can't control:

all that happens in the *tomorrows to come*.

Please read this with all the tenderness and compassion that fills me as I type.

Today may not be what we want. It may not include all the people we thought would be right by our side in this season. It may be that many of our dreams didn't come true. We've lost a lot. We've grieved a lot. And now we have a collection of heartbreaking memories we wish we didn't have. We also have memories we wish we could make, but things didn't quite work out that way.

It hurts. We don't understand. So how could any of this be answered prayer?

Because God isn't done.

A big step forward is to receive what is good about this day and what is hard about this day without a clenched jaw and a racing heart. There may be some things we can change today. And there will be a lot we can't. But instead of trying to control the uncontrollable, we can quiet that angst with a beautiful practice called *surrender*.

The quicker we surrender to God what we don't understand, the less we will suffer. And each day we accept our life and surrender to God what we cannot control, our trust in Him will grow and produce the fruit of peace.

Trying to control the uncontrollable breeds chaos. Surrendering to the only One in control produces peace.

Let's restate those last two sentences: Controlling others breeds chaos. Surrendering to God produces peace.

Control is our way of trying to perfect that which will never be perfected.

Control is our way of trying to reduce the risk of getting hurt, but it actually increases relational tensions.

Control is our way of trying to keep things the way we want them to be, not realizing how that stress is making us fall apart in the process. And it is at the exact place where we are controlling that we send the clearest of signals to others and to God that we don't trust them.

Like I said before, that which we don't trust, we will try to control. And what an exhausting way to live. Anxious. Annoyed. Angry. Irritable. Discontented. And acting like we have power that we won't ever have. I am realizing that when I live this way, I am succumbing to self-centered and fear-based living. It's not God-centered and freedom-based living.

I'm not saying you and I are blatantly self-centered people. I'm saying when we remove trusting God from the center of our perspective, that vacuum will be filled with an elevated sense that everything depends on us.

Remember the two crucial sentences? Control breeds chaos. Surrender produces peace.

The only way I have found to stop myself from some of the controlling actions mentioned is to recognize when I'm getting controlling. And in that moment of realization, I need to pause and declare I'm making the choice to begin surrendering to God that which is beyond my ability to change in the moment.

- "God, I'm surrendering this unexpected turn of events. Instead of panicking and missing Your provision, I'm going to look for Your provision that is here."
- "God, I'm surrendering this tension with my friend. Instead of rushing to make judgments against her or myself, I'm going to let the Jesus in me talk to the Jesus in her through prayer before addressing this issue."
- "God, I'm surrendering my doubts that You are really going to come through for me this time. Instead of looking at today's circumstances as evidence of Your absence, I'm going to trust that today is a necessary part of the process only You can see right now."
- "God, I'm surrendering how sad I feel today. Instead of trying to numb out in unhealthy ways, I'm going to get myself

somewhere I can worship, listen to Your truth, look for Your presence in nature, or process this with people who are biblically wise."

These prayers are my way of acknowledging that God leads and I follow. Now, please note that I used the word *surrendering*, which indicates I'm still in the process of doing this. I have in no way perfected this, but I am willing to practice it. Some days you'll find me doing better than others. God already knows how flawed my efforts will be, but keeping my heart bent toward Him more times than I pull away from Him is good progress.

I was doing this surrender exercise during a recent mission trip to Nicaragua. On a day that we had a lot planned, somehow the car we were driving locked us out automatically when we shut the door. We had quickly jumped out of the car to take a picture. We left our belongings, including the keys, inside, not realizing that when we closed the door it would lock on its own.

That one mistake cost us an entire day. Everything we had planned got derailed because where we were, there were no locksmiths. Someone had to drive four hours round trip to go get an extra set of keys.

It was an especially hot day. We missed out on lunch. The dust of passing vehicles was slowly covering every inch of us. And we were utterly helpless and stranded until we got that extra set of keys. I remember feeling so frustrated and annoyed. And I could feel a pretty bossy attitude coming on. The thought of surrendering this to God felt ridiculous. (Sidenote: in the midst of real-life angst, if it feels ridiculous to surrender something to God, that's a sign it's the absolute right thing to do.)

I was praying while walking to find some sort of a bathroom when all of a sudden I noticed little white flowers moving in a perfectly straight line. It looked like the flowers had sprouted feet and were just moving and grooving along the edge of a cement wall. I thought to myself, *Have I gotten so overheated today that now I'm delirious enough to think there are white flowers dancing in front of me?* When I bent down to look more closely, I realized there were ants underneath each flower. They were carrying flowers three times as big as them with seemingly no struggle at all.

The flowers were moving in the right direction because the ants were strong enough to carry them. The ants were doing what the flowers could never do on their own. It was such a beautiful picture of how it should look when I surrender to God what I cannot figure out or work out on my own.

I whispered a prayer under my breath. "God, I am so frustrated that we have wasted an entire day. There was so much good that could have been accomplished today. But I am making the choice to surrender this frustration to You and trust that this is exactly where You wanted us right now. Even though it feels like a pointless waste of time, I know there's more to this event than I can see."

And that's when it dawned on me. I had prayed and asked God to protect us on this trip. I knew in that moment that, somehow, trusting Him meant believing that this car situation represented us living in the answered prayers for His protection.

How many times in my life has God answered my prayers, but because His answers don't look like I expect them to look, I grumble and complain? How many times have these kinds of incidents happened that could have served to deepen my trust in the Lord, but I was too focused on my frustration to make the connection? How many times have I created chaos with people I love because I would rather control them than trust them? How many times have I feared being disappointed by God so much that I treated praying to Him like a last resort rather than my first priority?

Surrender isn't a one-time event at the time of our salvation. Surrendering is daily. Sometimes it's hourly or even moment by moment. Throughout the Bible we find instances where God acts, and that action is a starting point that has to be faithfully walked out. For instance, God saved the Israelites from Egypt. But the Israelites had to walk out the reality of their freedom by learning how to leave Egypt behind them as they walked into the promised land of God. The apostle Paul tells us to "work out [our] salvation with fear and trembling" (Philippians 2:12). He was saying yes, we are saved by Jesus, and that salvation has implications we have to walk out and work out.

The same concept is true of surrender. We have to learn to surrender and then learn how to continually surrender to God. So it's less about surrender with a period at the end. It's more about surrender*ing* that leaves us in process, a continuing action that has to be consistently tended to because it is an action that has started but is incomplete. It's in process and that is totally okay, as long as we keep the process going. How do we keep the surrendering going? Well, it's choosing to hand over to God what I want to control.

It's not an act of weakness. It's actually a strength I need to develop more and more. My job is to stay self-controlled and be obedient to God. God's job is everything else.

I know releasing our grip on wanting to control narratives and outcomes and anything that could further complicate our lives can feel like free-falling. I also know it's tempting to say, "Surrendering is not going to fix this situation. Nope, it's just going to lead to more hurt, more damage, and more chaos. I've seen it happen time and time again. That's what I'm trying to avoid."

I. Understand. Completely.

And so does God.

This is not a book that is leading you to sign up for more hurt. This is not a book where I'm telling you not to act responsibly, not to create safeguards in your life. But when you think about it, while safeguards often work, we can never say we've created a completely safe world. A world where every situation and person is 100 percent safe and trustworthy. A world where we'll never, ever be hurt again. That's just not how life works.

Of course, we want to be wise, be aware, and take action to prevent abusive or unsafe behaviors from going unchecked. But let's go back to that idea of surrendering, where the "ing" ending to this verb tells us it's progressive. It's an ongoing work in our lives.

We get to decide the ways we practice that surrendering. So if surrendering feels like you're simply signing up for more hurt, maybe you need to start small.

One of the things I've learned to do is this: the very minute I feel anxiety or feelings of wanting to grab control or feelings of distrust rising, I pause and ask myself, *How can I practice surrendering—this very minute?*

What does that look like in real life?

Surrendering looks like . . .

- Whispering a short surrender prayer to God.
- Praying with my hands open.
- Writing down the individual things I'm worried about on index cards and laying them all out on the floor. The ones I can realistically work on, I pick up. All the others, I tuck into my Bible.
- Setting a short time limit on my swirling thoughts when I'm trying to figure things out and I start to obsess and worry. I'll give myself ten minutes more, and then I change my environment and tell myself, *I've done my part for today. Now let God do His part for today.*
- I also like to put on worship music in the background as I'm doing some of these other acts of release. I recently found out that God designed our bodies in such a specific way that singing calms our anxiety. The voice box, the larynx, is connected to the vagus nerve, which means when we sing or even hum, it will help slow our heart rate and calm us down.[16] That just

brings me even more understanding of how much God cares for us in the most tender ways as we stay focused on Him.

- Lastly, we can make it a point to notice and call out the small delights of the day and credit God's goodness and faithfulness for all of it.

Doing these simple practices helps me stay in the process of surrendering my desire for control; my attachment to outcomes; my never-ending questions, doubts, and fears . . . all into the hands of the God who is always faithful. The God who personally goes before me. The God who never leaves us to figure it all out on our own.

The more I trust Him to do what only He can do, the less I will resist Him. The less I resist Him, the less I will suffer with anxiety about the unknown.

Trusting God will give us the courage to trust others who deserve it. When we live surrendered to Him, we know we will eventually be okay even when others break our confidence. Trusting God should be the solid and certain foundation upon which we can stand as we take the risk and enjoy the rewards of relationships.

As I trust God more and more, I won't panic nearly as much about the fear of the unknown in my relationships. I can feel the anxiety but not be ruled by it when I turn each moment of confusion into a moment of surrender.

One More Thing I Want You to Know

I was scrolling through Instagram recently when a post by Nicki Koziarz grabbed my attention. She was teaching on the definition of the word *manna*, the food God provided for the Israelites when they were wandering in the desert.[17] It prompted me to get my Bible and read the story again in Exodus 16. I am in a completely different season of life now than I was the last time I read this section of Scripture. And wow, as my eyes danced across the thin pages of my Bible, I noticed new details that hit me differently now.

The Israelites had been desperate for this deliverance. They were being beaten and worked mercilessly by the Egyptians. But when God sent them a message through Moses, promising to bring them to the land He swore to give to Abraham, Isaac, and Jacob, they were too discouraged and exhausted to hope for deliverance. The Bible tells us, "Moses reported this to the Israelites, but they did not listen to him because of their discouragement and harsh labor" (Exodus 6:9).

I relate to these feelings. Harsh relational realities, betrayals, deep disappointments, hard-to-accept circumstances, and big life things not working out like I hoped they would—these can make it difficult for me to see past my current realities. I tend to trust that things won't get better more than I trust that they will. When circumstances don't look like we imagined answered prayers should look like, it's easy to miss God all together.

This happened over and over with the Israelites. And it happens over and over with me. Instead of letting faith fill in the gaps of the unknowns of my life, I am much more prone to get discouraged, doubtful, and to whisper under my breath, "This is just the way things go for me. Why do I even bother to pray?"

I don't like typing that. I don't like living like that.

That's why Nicki's Instagram post about the food (manna) God provided for the Israelites when they were finally delivered and free in the desert really grabbed my attention. She explained that the word *manna* means "what is this?"

And there it was, a detail I never knew before but desperately needed to learn right now. Because how many times has God given me His perfect provision based on His precise knowledge of what I needed, and I looked at it with eyes of confusion at best—or, at worst, I never noticed it at all? Manna falling all around me while I'm crying out to God, asking, *Why are these annoying white flakes falling all over me? What is this? God, make it go away! I trusted You to provide food and got this?!*

The very thing I want to brush off, rush through, and get so disappointed and discouraged by . . . once again . . . might be the exact answer, for today, to the prayers I've been praying.

Can you think of anything in your life right now where you've asked some version of the "what is this" question? Don't read past that question. It's an important one. Because when we stop surrendering to God, we start trying to take control.

I pray we will be brave enough to open our hearts and open our doors to surrender to God, so He can help us take those first steps of moving on. I want to trade the powerlessness of trying to control outcomes and people for the strength of surrender. I want to release my fears and replace them with a beautiful sense of wonder. And I want to start walking forward, believing there are still good people worth trusting. God is still good and has good things in store for me. Life is still a beautiful gift. And there's a great big, amazing world that exists just beyond my front door.

Remember:

- Humans who break our trust do not have the power to break apart God's good plans for our lives.
- That which we don't trust, we'll try to control.
- While it's good to plan for the future, we don't want to obsess over the future.

- This is what I can control: making wise choices today. This is what I can't control: all that happens in the tomorrows to come.
- Controlling others breeds chaos. Surrendering to God produces peace.

Receive:

"The steadfast love of the LORD never ceases;
  his mercies never come to an end;
they are new every morning;
  great is your faithfulness."
  (Lamentations 3:22–23 ESV)

"Therefore do not worry about tomorrow, for tomorrow will worry about itself. Each day has enough trouble of its own." (Matthew 6:34)

Reflect:

- What kinds of things do you find yourself doing in an attempt to "make sure" things turn out well for yourself and others?
- In what area of your life are you obsessing over the future instead of simply planning for the future? What steps could you take today to place your trust in God to handle what tomorrow holds?
- What thoughts come to mind when you sit with and ponder the following statements? "Controlling others breeds chaos. Surrendering to God produces peace."

Pray:

Heavenly Father,

You know how I wrestle between trusting You versus taking control. I need Your guidance as I seek to surrender it all to You. I want to trade the powerlessness of trying to control outcomes and people for the strength of surrender. I want to release my fears and replace them with a peaceful trust in You. And I want to start walking forward, believing there are still good and safe people in this world worth connecting with. I can't do this without You.

In Jesus' name, amen.

Chapter Nine

Ice Makers and Oceans

•

It was just a broken ice maker. It wasn't a catastrophic event. I was safe. I was in a good place. And I was looking forward to spending a few days on vacation. But when the ice maker broke at the beach house we were staying in and I couldn't find a repairman to help me, I started spiraling. I was having an out-of-proportion reaction to the minor situation in front of me. And when that happens, I know it's not just about the thing. It's all the other things attached to this thing.

I could feel the tears coming. Soon, I had my fist in the air and the fussing began.

"If only he wouldn't have broken my trust over and over. If only I hadn't been so enabling. Then maybe our relationship would still be intact, and I wouldn't feel so stinkin' frustrated every time something breaks, because he knows how to fix things! I can't fix this thing! And I can't find a repairman. And even if I do find someone to help me, what if a part has to be ordered? And what if that part is on back order? Or, worse yet, what if it can't be fixed? So now here I am with another broken thing, and there's nothing I can do about it!"

I know. I was acting like a child. As I mentioned, I'm usually very "go with the flow." But not this day.

About the third time I said out loud, "I can't fix this ice maker!" I stopped myself. I suddenly felt incredibly embarrassed by my tantrum. But instead of making me stop, the embarrassment only increased the intensity of my frustration. I let out a guttural "ugggghhhhhhh!" Suddenly, it was almost as though emptying my tightening throat of all the anger had made space for a thought. Five words popped into my head . . . *But what if I could?*

What if I tried to fix it? What's the worst thing that could happen—it breaks? It was already broken.

I rolled my eyes at the absurdity of what I was about to attempt. I googled "how to fix an ice maker." It was too general of a search with way too many options and way too many written instructions. Then I decided to YouTube my question, and I narrowed my search with the name of the fridge.

I watched the video several times. I opened the freezer where all the mechanics for the ice maker were housed. I might have said out loud, "You will not defeat me. By golly, I'm going to figure this thing out."

And, no joke, I did! I fixed that ice maker! You would have thought I just climbed Mount Everest or finished running a marathon based on the way I did a victory dance around that kitchen!

And when I heard the ice turn and fall into my glass, I realized it was never really about the ice maker or me fixing it. It was a moment of resilience I could see, touch, and celebrate. This resilience was tangible evidence that I was healing, growing, and moving forward by trying new things. But most of all, it was a moment when I didn't succumb to the limitations of living hurt.

I've written in my journal so many times, "Just because I've been hurt doesn't mean I have to live hurt." That's easy to write. Hard to live out. But in this moment, fresh out of breath from all my dancing, I was doing it!

What does this have to do with rebuilding trust? When you have your trust broken, part of what feels so incredibly unfair and hard to get through is how much it takes from you. Broken trust diminishes relationships, opportunities, the feeling of freedom you once felt when things seemed safe and secure. Skepticism starts to set in, not just with the person who broke your trust but with other people as well. We've already looked at that. But another thing that happens is we put limitations on ourselves as a result of another person's actions.

I won't assign this to you, but for me, the biggest limitation holding me back after experiencing a lot of broken trust was that I became so focused on what I lost, I couldn't see what I could gain. I didn't know how to move forward with myself. I didn't know how to rebuild my resilience muscles. I didn't know how to get unstuck from the trauma. I didn't want the betrayal and lies that had been spoken over me in the past to become liabilities in my future.

Now, what does all of this have to do with the ice maker I fixed and with building my resilience muscles? A big component of my trust issues is the trauma I experienced because of how I was deceived and all the gaslighting and cover-ups created by those who betrayed me. As I said earlier, each time, I knew something was off, but when I sought clarification, I was made to feel like I was the crazy one. It felt so jarring. Unsettling. Disorienting. This kind of deception is emotional abuse. But I didn't know that. I didn't realize all the damage it was doing. The story I kept telling myself was that something was wrong with me.

Maybe for you, trust issues revolve around smaller breaches in trust. Maybe you found out your friend has been gossiping behind your back. Maybe your coworker took credit for something you worked on. Maybe your mom said she was too busy with work to come see your daughter's ballet recital, but you found out she was actually going to a concert with your brother.

Whether the event that fractured your trust was big, like a betrayal, or smaller, how you process these events will affect how you do or do not move forward.

For me, I was too unsure of what was and wasn't happening, so I kept quiet about it all. I feared that bringing others into my suspicions could only further damage increasingly fragile relationships and possibly expose me as the one who was no longer in touch with reality. What if I accused this person of lying, but then, when others were brought in, the problem was really me and not them? Who would want to help me if I was the crazy, suspicious one making false accusations?

I kept quiet. And I sank deeper and deeper into despair.

One therapist who specializes in trauma said, "Trauma isn't an event that happens. It's how you process the event."[18] So, if you process it in a healthy way, with a strong support system that helps you heal and see the truth more clearly, then the lasting effects won't be as devastating. But if you don't have that help as you experience a traumatic event, then you could end up feeling stuck in that trauma.

I believe the trauma stuck with me because I had kept silent about what was happening and I had no one to process with or receive care from. The story of betrayal wasn't just an event in my life; it became the story that messed up my life. When our processing of an event is limited to just our own perspective, tainted by hurt, shock, and heartbreak, it's like trying to look through shattered glass. Clarity isn't a gift that shattered glass will ever give you. Everything looks jagged and broken and dangerous.

The betrayals happened to me. But the trust issues were happening in me.

When you feel you have no voice, no support, no protection, and no clarity, broken trust turns into trust issues.

The betrayals happened to me.

But the trust issues were happening in me.

No one else could change this for me. I had to decide to do that.

New relationships, safer people, better

circumstances, and healthier environments could all play a part in me moving forward. However, the parts deep inside me that were filled with simmering frustrations, that were focused on the unfairness and fixated on the awful chain of events set off because of betrayals? Those are the parts that had me stomping around the kitchen with a clenched fist and a limited belief that broken ice machines and brokenness in general were just my plight in life.

I know this is a whole lot of drama around what should have been just the everyday aggravation of a household appliance not working. But isn't this where a lot of us fall apart? It's that last little broken thing, put on top of all the weight of the hurt we're carrying, that breaks us wide open and leaks out another flood of tears.

Figuring out how to deal with these issues inside me felt so complicated and exhausting. Plus, I know unhealed trauma attracts unhealed trauma. We are drawn to what is familiar. And the last thing I wanted to do was to be unintentionally drawn toward people who cope with life using deceptive tactics. I didn't want another relationship where this was the case. And even more so, I didn't want to start being deceptive as a way to self-protect.

I had to get a plan. And the plan couldn't be to have my counselor on speed dial 24-7 forever.

That moment in the kitchen when I rebelled against the brokenness and fixed that ice maker taught me something big. And I knew this rebellious act of resilience was going to be an important part of helping me move forward.

If how I processed the betrayal was part of what got me into this mess, then reprocessing could surely help me find a way to get unstuck and out of this mess.

Two words that indicated stuck-ness to me were *can't* and *don't*.

> *I* can't *deal with this. I* can't *do this. I* can't *trust people. I* can't *fix this. I* can't *change.*
> *I* don't *think this is ever going to get better. I* don't *want to try. I*

don't *believe it's possible. I* don't *think God has a good plan for me. I* don't *want to hope again.*

Now, please lean in close here. If we don't tend well to this kind of broken processing, our can'ts and don'ts will turn into won'ts.

I won't *deal with this.*
I won't *do this.*
I won't *trust people.*
I won't *fix this.*
I won't *change.*
I won't *get better.*
I won't *try.*
I won't *believe.*
I won't *trust that God has a good plan.*
I won't *hope again.*

Healing from betrayal and trust issues will be layered and can be complicated. It will take time. Probably more time than any of us will want it to. But by listening for our "I can'ts" and "I don'ts" and making sure they don't turn into "I won'ts," we can see significant progress today.

Maybe try using some new words like,

I am willing to try.
Maybe I can find someone who can teach me.
This is an opportunity for me to be brave.
I can do this.

Or, like me,

But what if I could?

My counselor loves to remind me that words frame our reality. If we believe we can't, chances are we won't.

Now, one last thing. This realization wasn't just limited to me fixing that ice maker. No, I need to listen for the "I can'ts" and "I don'ts" each and every day.

On that same trip, some friends joined me at the beach. Ann came from Canada, and Jessica came from Tennessee. Ann and I were basically on the same page with our definition of what "going to the beach with friends" meant. It was all beach chairs and reading and processing life and eating good food and playing cards. Jessica liked all those things too. But to her, going to the beach meant getting in the ocean.

Excuse me, what?! You mean that giant body of water that is so very lovely to look at but also contains jellyfish that sting, sharks that bite, and stingrays that jab holes through flesh?

Jess was being such a funny, funny girl pretending like she really wanted Ann and me to risk life and limb while also getting our hair wet and our bathing suits full of sand.

Oh, but she actually was serious. And no matter how much we protested, she still carried down three boogie boards to the ocean. *Sweet thing. Bless her for wasting so much energy.*

When we got down near the water, Jessica didn't say a word. She just laid a boogie board near our toes and took off to jump into the waves.

"I don't do oceans," I mumbled under my breath.

Shoot—as soon as I heard myself say "don't," I rolled my eyes. I let out a big sigh and shook off the protests of all the cells of my body telling me to stop, freeze, and sit back down right this minute. I grabbed the boogie board and went flying and flapping into the white foam coming at me with more force than I expected. Nothing was graceful, as the water twisted my body sideways and pulled my bathing suit bottom down. In all the craziness of trying not to show my unmentionables to the world, I started laughing harder than I'd laughed in a good long while. I stayed in the water and played and jumped and had the time of my life. Best of all, I didn't die! But I sure did live those moments of my life to their absolute fullest.

It was another step, or maybe a leap, forward.

Please try this. I mean, you don't have to fix an ice maker or jump into an ocean, but don't miss an opportunity to overcome an "I can't" or "I don't" today. You will see progress today. You will build your resilience muscles today. And over time, the more capable you feel, the more empowered you will feel. The more empowered you feel, the more you'll trust your own discernment again. The more you trust your own discernment, the less you'll fear the risk of inviting the right imperfect people in. The less you'll resist trying to rebuild, rediscover, and remake your life that is so worth living. Really living. Not just barely making it through. But better than it's ever been.

How do I know that? Because we are growing. And growing means we are living. And living means there's more good that God wants us to participate in. Continuing to pursue relationships is risky. But the greater and more tragic risk is pulling inside of ourselves and giving up.

The people who have hurt me can't make me give up. That's my choice. They can't make you give up either. That's your choice.

So I choose ice makers and oceans and living.

One More Thing I Want You to Know

Being brave is not always something you feel. It's something you do.

You do it in the face of fear and unknown outcomes and risks you don't really want to take.

You do it when your enemy is staring you down with taunting statements of defeat. You do it not to prove there's something great inside you. You do it because if you don't, something will die inside you.

Being brave is not always something you *feel*. It's something you *do*.

You do brave things because it's time to rise up and speak up and let truth find its freedom with your voice.

What happened was wrong. Acknowledge it. Speak it. Cry over it. But don't die over it. You've been hurt, but you don't have to live hurt.

You do brave things because you were made to connect. Not with all people but with the right people. Take the right risks. Take it slow. But don't stop. Don't withdraw. Don't disappear.

You do brave things because you are a woman who can kneel humbly and rise intentionally. You will find good people, and good people will find you.

And you'll do brave things until you become brave. You'll know love again. You'll know laughter again. And you'll know deep in your bones that you won't waste all that you've learned. Those spilled tears, every one of them, helped you let go of the pain to make room for possibility.

Your life is not a tragedy. It's a testimony that God is your Rock and your Redeemer. And if your hands are shaking, let it be only because you're pointing at the devil, who picked the wrong girl to mess with this time.

Don't wait until you feel brave. Go be brave. Remember: if God is for you, there is nothing that can stand against you (Romans 8:31).

Remember:

- Trying new things in small acts of resilience is tangible evidence of healing, growing, and moving forward.
- If we believe we can't, chances are we won't.
- The betrayals happened to me. But the trust issues were happening in me.

- Continuing to pursue relationships is risky. But the greater and more tragic risk is pulling inside of ourselves and giving up.
- Being brave is not always something you feel. It's something you do.

Receive:

"What, then, shall we say in response to these things? If God is for us, who can be against us?" (Romans 8:31)

Reflect:

- What are some small acts of resilience that have made you feel strong and brave recently?
- What "I don't" and "I can't" statements could you start working to overcome today?

Pray:

Heavenly Father,

Some of the oceans I see in front of me feel dangerous and too risky to comprehend—let alone tiptoe into. But I know You are placing opportunities before me where I can practice small acts of resilience with Your loving and watchful eye on me. Help me do good, brave things, especially in the seasons where I don't feel brave at all.

In Jesus' name, amen.

Chapter Ten

The Secret to Really Healing

•

If I ever tell you I went on a hike, I don't want you to picture the steep-incline, sweating-and-coughing-up-a-lung kind of hike. Some people call that fun. I don't. Oh, I've done those kinds of ridiculous hikes when my friends who talked me into doing it assured me that it's not "that hard." And "You'll get to the top pretty quickly and the scenery is so worth it." And "Oh no, there are definitely no bears." Liar, liar, pants on fire. The scenery really was beautiful, but there are less risky and more reasonable hikes to be found that are more like a gentle walk through the woods, where you will also discover beautiful things.

The gentle walk kind of hike was what I was on when I saw a little plaque marking a fallen tree. I thought the tree was dead. The sign placed in front of the tree said, "The Resilient Oak Tree: The storm that felled this tree didn't stop it from protecting both the forest and island community with its thriving canopy."

What a beautiful legacy for a tree. I loved that. Though the storm knocked the tree down, the tree was still able to help protect the community.

But as I kept looking, I better understood its name. The tree wasn't dead. Even though the big roots were pulled up with a large section of dirt still attached, somehow, part of the tree trunk touching the ground grew new roots where it fell. And the upper part of the tree is still thriving to this day.

As I stood there looking at the tree, the picture of resiliency it portrayed spoke to me personally. When we have our trust broken in big ways, it can feel like we're in the middle of a fierce and mighty storm. I would love to say that in my situation I was so firmly planted with deep roots that the broken trust bent me but didn't break me.

But that's just not true.

The hurricane-force winds continued on in my life for so many years, it eventually knocked me down. Remember, I didn't just have my trust broken in one significant relationship; it seemed to keep happening in big ways and small ways over and over. I remember telling my friends I was knocked so low that I felt as if I was licking the floor of hell. I didn't know how to get back up.

Days turned into weeks, and then the weeks turned into months of such deep heartbreak and suffering that I hardly had the energy to do much else except to just survive. I was doing what I had to do with my kids and my job, but something deep down inside me felt dead, numb, and indifferent. I didn't want to let that part of me come to life again, because if I allowed myself to feel anything, intense pain would be right there waiting to tear me apart. Having no feelings seemed better than to open myself up to that feeling.

Eventually, the numbness wore off and extreme loneliness set in. I could no longer stuff it down and just go through the motions to survive. The pain was demanding I deal with the brokenness inside me.

I didn't know how to force the part of me so bent over and broken to stand back up, replant my roots, and try to be like I was before. This trauma had changed so much about my life. And honestly, I was changed. I felt damaged, broken, and remade, but not for the better.

But, as I stared at the place where the fallen tree had grown new roots, I found it to be one of the most beautiful trees I had ever seen. There were many huge oak trees on this trail, but none of the others spoke to me like this one. Its message of resiliency was so inspiring that I stood there for a long time, admiring and honoring what the tree had done.

I found it interesting that the fallen tree hadn't separated itself from the old roots. You could still see them lifted up, out of the ground. So, the tree hadn't lost who it once was, but it had gained new life by planting new roots. This didn't happen overnight. But it did happen. It looked way different than it had before, but it was a good different. Before, it looked like a big tree. Now, it wasn't just a tree; it was a tree with a message that inspired all who saw it.

Maybe the secret to really healing is to change the end goal. Instead of expecting the healing work to return me back to how I was before, I could let the healing make me into a healthier version of myself. Instead of focusing on all that was taken from me, maybe I could shift my focus to what this new season could give me. And best of all, maybe, like the tree, one of the best things I could gain in this process was a story that could help other people through the scary seasons of being betrayed by friends and loved ones.

I never wanted the story of my life to be that I'm the divorced Bible teacher. I never wanted to lose the friends I've lost. I never wanted to have people judge me, ridicule me, make up stories about me, or dismiss me, as though divorce is emotional leprosy. But as I stood staring at that tree, I thought to myself, *They may have knocked me down, but I will accept what happened, grow new roots, and turn broken into beautiful.*

Instead of focusing on all that was *taken from me*, maybe I could shift my focus to what this new season *could give me*.

And that's when I realized the real antidote for trust issues. It isn't to perfectly choose the right people. It isn't to catch every rip and make sure it is repaired perfectly. The real solution is to accept that trust isn't ever a guarantee with humans. Some relationships will hurt us. Some relationships will help heal us. But if we anchor our hope to the Lord, the risks of trust will be much less terrifying as we develop the muscles of resiliency.

The woman who thrives in life isn't the one who never has her heart broken. It's the one who plants her brokenness in the rich soil of her faith in God and waits with anticipation to see what good thing God will grow next. Psalm 1:3 tells us, "That person is like a tree planted by streams of water, which yields its fruit in season and whose leaf does not wither—whatever they do prospers." Nothing we ever place in God's hands will be returned without meaning.

Don't be scared by the storms that bust up your trust. Because you know what's more powerful than destructive storms? The person who rises back up from what tried to take her out. That's God's girl. And she is not here to fall down and stay down. *Hey, Devil, you mess with her and God's going to use her testimony to mess you up and take you out.*

Friend, you are stronger than you know. You are wiser than you give yourself credit for. You are more alive today than ever before. Now, dare to trust again. Do it carefully, and give it wisely. But don't put the pressure on yourself to do this trust thing perfectly. God will be right there with you. And, as we've learned together, no one is more powerful than God.

Some of your people will be trustworthy, and some will not. But you, my friend, are now well prepared to do the best you can and keep on walking. And the next time we bump into each other, I hope we both have stories of relationships with loved ones that are safe, healthy, and much more peaceful. And that we are able to wisely and confidently tell the right people, "I want to trust you, and now I do."

One More Thing I Want You to Know

What does healing and trusting again look like?

It looks like tears
Facing fears
Crawling back in bed
Covers over my head
It looks like time
Admitting I'm not fine
Not yet and no clue when
Wanting to give up
But not giving up
It looks like a fight
Staring up at midnight
A cold bed
Jumbled thoughts
Emotions both numb and wild
Deciding to live
Refusing to give . . . over to defeat
It's not a checklist
Or a clenched fist
Or an attempt to barely exist
No, healing is living
It's rebellious acts of resilience
It's chasing the sun
Rediscovering fun
It's climbing back up
Maybe clawing my way up
And through

And out
Refusing to entertain defeating doubt
It's working through what I'm walking through
And when another person breaks my trust
I won't let it break me
It's counseling and pondering
It's being okay with quiet
And then dancing it out so loudly
Lifting my head proudly
Kneeling to God humbly
And finally knowing I will be okay
Better than okay
Maybe my best ever
Definitely my best ever

Remember:

o Instead of focusing on all that was taken from me, maybe I could shift my focus to what this new season could give me.
o Nothing we ever place in God's hands will be returned without meaning.
o You are stronger than you know, wiser than you give yourself credit for, and more alive today than ever before.

Receive:

"That person is like a tree planted by streams of water,
which yields its fruit in season
and whose leaf does not wither—
whatever they do prospers." (Psalm 1:3)

I WANT TO TRUST YOU, BUT I DON'T

Reflect:

- After reading the story of the fallen oak tree, how were you inspired to notice the new roots you've been growing lately or to put down some new roots starting now?
- What was the most encouraging part of this chapter for you? What made it meaningful?

Pray:

Heavenly Father,

You have been so faithful to me and present with me as I've taken the time to learn more about trust in my relationships with You and the people in my life. You've never left me, and for that I'm grateful. Help me take to heart and prayerfully and wisely implement what I've learned. Show me the way forward—I trust You fully to be my guide and my steady help.

In Jesus' name, amen.

Conclusion

One More Thing God Wanted Me to Know

•

What you're about to read is a blog post I wrote fifteen years before I wrote this book. But I didn't remember it until someone recently found it and brought it to me. As I read it, my mouth fell open and I started shaking my head.

If you read my book *Good Boundaries and Goodbyes*, you know that book ended with a friend finding my childhood Bible and figuring out a way to get it to me, even though we hadn't seen each other in over thirty years. Inside the Bible there was a message I'd written as a teen that was exactly what I needed to read on the day I got the Bible back. It was the last confirmation that I was doing the right thing with one of the hardest decisions of my life.

And now, as I'm finishing this book, another note from my past self.

If this seems crazy, I agree. But isn't it just like God to use something so unexpected?

By Lysa. Written in 2009.

I have a friend whose life used to be like a treasured love letter. Each day she'd open up the well-creased paper and live out the gentle familiarity with great joy.

Her life read of love, purpose, tradition, stability, respect, and faith. Day by day, layer upon layer, her legacy decorated the edges of her love letter with strokes of consistent beauty.

Then, one shocking day, she awoke to find someone she trusted very much had knowingly and willfully torn her love letter in half. Shocked and hurt, she asked this someone to tape it back together.

Though the letter would never quite look the same, eventually a heart of forgiveness and eyes of grace allowed her to see the letter as lovely once more. Her little letter had been through a lot but, strangely enough, didn't seem as fragile as it had years before. The paper felt more stable than it had ever felt. And she found that good could even come from the rips and tears of life.

Healing days turned into healing years, and soon the paper's scar faded so much you could hardly tell it had been torn.

There was joy. But then sorrow returned.

One morning she awoke to find her letter missing. Frantic and desperate, she threw open her front door, gasping for air. And there, to her great horror, she saw bits and pieces of her letter swirling and being carried away in the wind. Her letter, her life, everything precious and seemingly protected, was never to be the same again.

This time it wasn't just tattered and torn. It was shredded beyond repair. She collapsed in a heap of tears. Grief like she'd never known overtook her. She went to bed and thought she'd stay there forever.

The days were suddenly dark. The nights were way too long. The hours seemed to creep along in torturous spans. Each minute so painful she wondered how much longer her heart could continue its beat-by-beat rhythm.

Then one day she willed herself out of bed. Maybe it was the longing for her letter of old. Maybe it was wishful thinking. Maybe it was the purest form of raw hope. She walked outside among the pieces and parts of her life's letter. Ragged edges on each torn piece spoke loudly of the state of the circumstances she couldn't escape. But, looking closely, she discovered something wondrous. Though the torn-apart letter couldn't be read in sentences and paragraphs, the individual words were still clear.

Piece by piece, she picked up the fragments of paper and read them one word at a time. So many of the words were glorious. Absolutely glorious. Her life was still there.

And though the letter would never be read exactly the same as it had, for the first time in a long while she saw beauty. Gathering the pieces together, she started lining them up in rows. Old words, new sentences.

The letter of her life took on a new meaning. All the truth that seemed to be shredded with the old letter was still there.

Truth still meant truthful. Full of truth.

Grace still meant graceful. Full of grace.

Joy still meant joyful. Full of joy.

And beauty still meant beautiful. Full of beauty.

Which is exactly what God kept whispering to her, but she couldn't seem to understand how anything so broken could ever be made whole again. Sometimes whole doesn't mean put back together the exact right way. For if someone discovers fullness within each broken piece, each part takes on a wholeness of its own.

So, for the first time in a long while, she smiled. And while she never thought she could be happy with a letter read in pieces, one word at a time, she found the fullness in each word and rediscovered her life.

She closed every door to her old life, picked up her pieces, and in complete fullness walked on.

This is how my life played out. I can't remember what friend might have inspired this story. Was there a friend? Or did I just take creative liberties to write something from my heart that I had to get out?

How could I have written something so long ago that seems to foreshadow what I never imagined I would walk through? Did some deep place in my soul somehow know? Or did God in His mercy take my hands and gently guide my fingers to type up this vision of profound hope?

The other thing that astounds me is how much of the wording matches what I've written in this book. Phrases like "She woke to find that someone she trusted very much had knowingly and willfully . . . shocked and hurt her." There's also the mention of "rips and tears" and "sorrow and joy." She also "went to bed and thought she'd stay there forever." Though the wording isn't exactly the same, it's too close to be coincidental. And then the ending . . . only God could have planned the ending.

God made sure I saw this. And I am certain He intentionally showed it to me before I wrote these last words in the book, because He wanted you to see it as well.

He is trustworthy. He knows our story from beginning to end. He knows right where we are today. He is with you. And where God is, good is being worked out.

Hold tightly to Him. And keep on going, friend. There is a great big world out there. New joys I don't want you to miss. Beautiful sights to discover. And so many reasons to laugh and smile and enjoy the people you love.

My journey has shifted from grieving to proving to myself that I can still love my life and be brave enough to trust again. I'm grateful. I'm more whole. I'm ready to walk into this next season smiling. And when I do cry, I'll see it as my way to acknowledge that there were yesterdays I truly loved.

I can simultaneously honor some of the past memories that were good while walking toward an unknown but hope-filled future. As I wrote in my blog post, "old words, new sentences." The letter of my life truly has taken on new meaning. What threatened to break me only served to make me more determined. I will live this life God entrusted to me with integrity and gratitude and wonder. And I trust you will too.

Update from Lysa

.

The topic of trust is one that has been deeply personal to me, especially during the two years I took to research and write this book. As you know, I've experienced many unexpected life changes in the past decade. The most significant was the trauma of betrayal and—after years of unsuccessful work—the death of my marriage. But there were other relationships where trust was deeply broken. Some of those survived because of intentional repair work on both my part and theirs. Other relationships did not survive, which compounded my grief.

In the midst of all this, I had times when I wrestled deeply with not understanding what God was allowing. There were moments when I felt betrayed by God. But there were also moments when I felt closer to Him than ever.

The ironic part of my ever-changing life is that I like consistency. I like the feeling of getting life to a good place and keeping it peaceful. And yet, the way my story has played out has been anything but predictable.

I wrote this book as I was navigating so much life change and learning how to trust again. And I wanted to be authentic to the process I was going through. So, the way you experienced this book as a reader is the way I was experiencing everything in real time as the writer. I truly did not know if I would ever be able to date again, believe someone again, or love again, and I invited you into that struggle with me.

But there has been a beautiful new chapter in my story that I also want to share with you. After remaining single for several years, God brought an amazing man named Chaz into my life, and we knew what we'd found in each other was love. It's a beautiful love that requires work like love always does. And it's also a togetherness that is safe, honest, fun, funny, and surrendered to the sacred way the Lord tells us to love and care for each other. I referenced Chaz a few times throughout these pages as someone I was dating, but now I have the great honor of calling him my husband.

As always, I want to be honest with you here. Although I am incredibly happy and so very grateful for Chaz, my situation has not been tied up in a neat, nice bow. I've still been marked by the deep hurt of broken trust. I still sometimes wrestle with triggers and fears. But even with all these realities, I am living proof that it is possible to experience tremendous healing, to trust again . . . to love again . . . to believe God has a good plan and His faithfulness to us never changes.

Bonus Chapter

When the Organization That Should Have Helped Me Actually Hurt Me

•

"But do you have bruises? Or even a picture from a time when this person's actions caused bruises?" I couldn't believe what I was hearing on this phone call with a ministry friend I had known for a long time. I wanted to send her a picture from the surgery I'd had the year before.

I used to make myself look at it when the question *Am I crazy?* would play on repeat inside my head. When the bits and pieces of evidence of continued betrayal kept surfacing but my questions were met with accusations that I was seeing things or even making them up, stuffing my concerns felt like the only option. Until one day, I guess I stuffed a little too much. The physical toll caused by emotional trauma was enormous. My colon twisted around itself, cutting off the blood flow, and as a result, I had to have a large part of my colon removed. The doctor showed me the picture of what my insides looked like, and he asked me, "What's going on? The way your insides have twisted and shifted make it look like you've been in a serious car accident, but you're telling me that's not the case."

I shook my head. "No accident," I replied. And my mouth felt awkwardly stiff and dry. I looked at the picture from my surgery and then back at the doctor. I don't know why I felt I couldn't tell him. Here was a man who had just saved my life in surgery, and I just sat there frozen.

I kept the picture. It reminded me that I'm not crazy.

I imagined myself saying to my friend on the phone, *No, I don't have pictures of bruises, but I have a massive scar that runs hip to hip and then vertically halfway up my midsection. And I have a photo of the physical implications of serious emotional trauma. I almost died. Does that count?*

But my mouth couldn't form those words before she fired off more questions. "I mean, surely you know a relationship doesn't just fall apart. Are there times you instigated any of this because you were being disrespectful? What if you make it a point to go home and love him better, build him up with your words, and have more sex? I just think there are some things you could do better."

I bit my bottom lip really hard. My heart was beating as if I were running a marathon, yet I was sitting perfectly still. So still, in fact, I couldn't even blink.

For years, I had invested my heart and my time into helping this lady achieve her ministry goals. I had given and served and invested in her organization. I never thought they owed me anything in return. But surely our relationship meant more to her than what her words and her tone were now reflecting.

I pressed my fingers into the inside corners of my eyes. I didn't want the tears to come.

Before I even got on the phone with her, I knew this conversation would be challenging. She'd sent me an email informing me that her organization planned to promote the marriage retreat they were hosting using my broken marriage as an example.

I immediately requested a phone call. Now she kept pressing on with the questions about the bruises. The impression she gave me was that if there had been physical abuse, then they would reconsider running the ads. In other words, physical abuse was the only way in her mind to give me the benefit of the doubt and legitimize the separation and pending divorce. Please hear me: physical abuse is horrific. It is inexcusable and damaging on so many levels. But emotional abuse is too. Unfortunately, this is not always recognized.

The leader I was talking with had never been through what I was facing. She and her husband seemed happily married. Her whole ministry career had been focused on helping people work on their marriages and keep their families together. And the truth was, she and her organization had helped save many marriages after couples attended their retreats, read her books, and completed her Bible studies.

I always thought her ministry's work was good and honorable. I had respected her and this organization for years. I trusted them. And I made the assumption that they would be a safe place to turn to for help in this time of shock and heartbreak.

I was wrong.

Worse, this broken trust wasn't just with my friend on the phone. It was with an entire organization. So, it felt much bigger, in some ways much weightier too. That's part of what's so frustrating with organizational hurt. Businesses and churches and ministries and schools are made up of people. Sometimes it's just a person who hurt us. But many times that person doesn't act alone, which can make it seem like the whole organization is suddenly against you or at least supporting the leadership who is making hurtful choices.

She was the messenger, but she wasn't acting alone. I imagined there were others sitting in that marketing meeting, thinking up the tagline about my broken marriage. Even if it was only a few people, in that moment while we were talking, she seemed to have the support of all her people, and I felt so small and alone. It felt like a massive army coming against me. That's part of what makes organizational hurt so traumatizing. The power of a collective force coming against my one fragile heart felt void of human compassion.

It was like there was some kind of blindness that prevented a whole group of people, who seemed so trustworthy and solid, from seeing how cruel their actions were becoming. I guess when I decided I would no longer stay quiet about what I was experiencing in my marriage, they feared it would make them look bad since people knew we had attended their events and utilized their resources.

Not one time on that call were the actions of my soon-to-be-ex-husband addressed. Not one time did they ask what they could do to support me. But even then, there was no acknowledgment of wrongdoing, nor was there an apology.

Now, please hear me: you are reading my version of events without the perspective of anyone from the organization. They made a mistake with this situation, but in all fairness, they probably made thousands of other good choices through the years. Also, please don't get distracted by trying to assign what happened to me to organizations you think might be responsible. I've changed enough small details to help us stay focused on acknowledging what can happen within larger groups. My point here isn't to stir the pot on organizational hurt that we've probably all experienced before. I know you're likely bringing your own heartbreak, confusion, and questions to these pages. But I also know how tempting it is to want to get all riled up and come out swinging in the name of demanding wrongs be made right. I get it. But we don't want to address sin in ways that draw us into sinning.

My point is to acknowledge the deep disillusionment that can happen when leaders we trust fail us and to ask the question, *How do I better process this?* I don't want to be jaded and carry the hurt I experienced here into other places. I don't want to assign this distrust to others who don't deserve it.

At the same time, I don't want to be afraid to address some of the system-wide issues I'm aware of. For example, this organization I encountered is not the only place where there was a refusal to acknowledge that emotional abuse is as serious as it is and that it must be factored in when giving counsel. You may feel the same way about some of the issues you're concerned about.

I can hardly have a conversation with anyone these days without the topic coming up of how difficult it is to trust organizations. Employees are disillusioned with their companies. Church hurt seems to be at an all-time high. Charitable giving feels risky, because we aren't sure how the money will really be used. We wonder about the hidden agendas that people in positions of influence

We don't want to address sin in ways that draw us into sinning.

might have. Do social media influencers really like that product they are promoting? Do politicians really plan to fight to help the people once they are elected? Does that leader who teaches about integrity really live up to the same standard they are calling others to? Does that person building the organization really care about the cause they are promoting, or are they simply growing a platform to benefit themselves? Does my boss really want to see my career advance, or is that just an empty promise to get me to constantly go above and beyond to benefit their bottom line?

I don't know. Chances are, with most situations, as you peel back the layers of human motivation, it's never going to be as clear-cut as we want it to be.

And even if we were able to dissect the motivations of others, we would probably find it challenging to determine where the good ends and the selfish reasoning begins. Their actions may be a scrambled mix of a lack of awareness and skewed perspectives. There would probably be a bit of self-protection layered with selfish ambition. Then there may still be some good intentions. But when we are looking at something through the lens of our own hurt, chances are we'll be pretty blind to the good that is still there.

We could spend our whole lives trying to figure out why people and organizations did what they did. Or why they continue to do what they do. But honestly, what good would it do to pinpoint what we believe is the reason for their actions?

If we've been hurt, we won't agree with their reasons.

Organizational hurt is real. And it can fuel the flames of distrust within us so intensely that we call into question every other area of our lives. It can make us want to give up on the career we once loved, quit going to church, distance ourselves from the causes we once believed in, stop voting, stop giving, and start placing blanket negative assumptions on people who are still participating with the organizations that caused us pain.

At some point what hurts us the most is no longer just what happened. It's the story we tell ourselves about what happened and the resignations we make afterward. They broke our trust. But they don't have the power to break us unless we decide we can't move on.

Can I make a sad admission that I really don't want to make? What the organization did to me in this instance paled in comparison to the hurt I then heaped on myself.

I played back the conversation dozens and dozens of times in my head. I felt incredibly justified in telling myself over and over what terrible people they were. I imagined calling them back, having an epic moment of satisfaction when I found just the right words to open their eyes to their wrongdoing, and finally hearing them say how wrong they were. I imagined them experiencing the same kind of betrayals I had experienced and then finally realizing how cruel their actions had been. I even imagined God Himself addressing them with a booming voice from heaven that sent them scrambling in fear.

And the more I let those thoughts run freely through my mind, the more I was turning into someone just as cruel as they were.

I started feeling justified in thinking things I don't normally think. To do things I wouldn't normally do. To say things I wouldn't normally say. To wish things on them I wouldn't normally wish on anyone. My thoughts eroded slowly, but the more I let them go unchecked, the more natural they felt.

Raw hatred started to feel natural. *God, help me.*

What started as distrust had turned into disgust.

And honestly, I had become just as hard-hearted and cruel to them as they ever were to me. What they had done was wrong. No doubt about it. But slinging back hate, even if it was only in my thoughts, was also wrong.

There's this picture I have in my mind when something hurtful happens. I imagine the Enemy delighting in humans hurting other humans. If we know Jesus, then Satan can't have our souls, but he sure loves to recruit good people with unresolved hurt in their hearts to do some of his work for him. In the spirit of C. S. Lewis's *The Screwtape Letters*, I sometimes think of what the Enemy might write in a letter instructing a demon about how to distract me from being the woman I want to be.

> You don't need to worry about recruiting her to do bad things. Just keep poking at her unresolved hurt, and she'll soon feel justified in doing and saying all kinds of things she wouldn't normally do or say. Fill the social media feed she looks at with images that make her feel intense feelings of how unfair her situation is. Feed her skepticism by surrounding her with others who don't trust organizations like the one that hurt her. Make her too distracted to open up God's Word, so she'll keep feeding on the lie that her bitterness protects her and her feelings of animosity aren't that big of a deal. Keep her blinded to the way she now walks around feeling on edge and on guard. As she gets more and more short-fused, impatient with the daily mistakes of others, give her a feeling of superiority that the issues are always someone else's fault.

Unresolved hurt inside us will be multiplied out by us unless we make the conscious choice to stop it.

So, can I ask you a tender question? Has there been a group of people or an organization you once trusted and respected who have hurt you like this?

It stinks. And whether your experience includes a hurtful conversation (like mine) or a conversation you would've liked to have had but never got the chance to, the pain lingers. I don't want to keep marching toward perspective changes before I fully acknowledge how hurtful these situations are.

What they did should not have happened. What was said to you and about you never should have been said. The way you gave and invested into that organization should have warranted more care and concern being extended to you. They shouldn't have broken your heart. They shouldn't have broken your trust. Leaders should have led better. Bosses should have cared for you better. Fellow Christians involved should have been honest, fair, kind, considerate, and loving. And with everything in me, I am so sorry they weren't. I am so sorry this whole hurtful situation ever occurred.

I'm not implying that any of this should be swept under a rug. If there are things with this group of people that need to be addressed, then as best as you can, address them. But don't let the people who hurt you now reduce your future down to the limitations of living hurt.

Just because this one ministry hurt me doesn't mean no ministry can be trusted.

Maybe the same is true in your situation too? I'm not asking you to sign on to this possibility yet. Just consider this as you read on. Remember, I'm here with you, wanting the best for you, and I understand there are lots of complexities with the situations that caused you a tremendous amount of pain. Part of what makes organizational hurt so challenging is that it can feel like they are the powerful ones. They just seem to move on without skipping a beat while we are desperately struggling. We want them to own what they did and make it right so that our world can tilt back into place and we can feel some sense of redemption.

Right?!

But what they do from here is completely out of our control. And if we hitch our ability to find peace to choices they may not ever make, we are in essence saying they get to control how we live from now on.

They don't deserve that kind of power over you.

What if you and I decided that enough has been taken from us? What might improve about your life and mine if we decided to accept the serenity that comes with moving on?

I know your brain might be firing off all the reasons why "just moving on" feels a bit like a slap in the face. I get it. But you know what would be the most tragic outcome of all? For the hurt they caused us to redirect us away from what's best for us. Yes, they broke our trust. But that shouldn't mean they broke us. We must not let what happened stop us from being the full, beautiful expressions of ourselves and who God made us to be.

Why would we want to give that kind of power to people running the organizations that already caused us pain? Why would we want that situation of pain to be the new determination of how we operate, what we believe, and how we view other people and other organizations? These hurtful experiences rightfully make us more careful not to jump blindly into a relationship with another similar organization. We can learn from our past experience and take that experiential insight with us as we move forward. But we can also exercise wisdom in not letting what happened lull us into one big blanket narrative that all similar organizations are run by bad people who are out to get what they want and then toss you aside.

I wish we were sitting together so you could see the deep compassion in my eyes and hear the tenderness in my voice right now.

Just because that church hurt you doesn't mean all churches are bad.

Just because some Christians let you down doesn't mean all Christians have ill intentions.

Just because this job went sideways and this boss was a jerk doesn't mean all leaders in your life should be treated with skepticism.

Just because this organization made a terrible judgment call doesn't mean all similar organizations should be avoided.

Just because those people didn't care well for your heart doesn't mean there aren't still amazing people out there who will treat you with love.

Ultimately, we must decide we are no longer interested in perpetuating the hurt. We may decide to help fix the issues. Or we may decide to move on from the issues. Either way, we must decide that, though the hurt came to us, we will no longer let it pass through us to others. We must decide that someone needs to be brave enough to tell the Enemy the division and animosity he has delighted in causing ends today. And that brave, brave person is the one staring back at you in the mirror. The very best way to refute the hurtful things others have said and done is for us to go on and live a great life.

The very best way to refute the hurtful things others have said and done is for us to go on and live a great life.

And you know what is necessary in order to live that great life? We must remember there are supernatural laws at play that are certainties we can count on. Just like we can count on the law of gravity to work—every time we drop something, it will fall—we can also count on God's law of sowing and reaping. What we decide to sow into our lives yields a harvest we will reap.

Galatians 6:7–10 reminds us,

> Do not be deceived: God cannot be mocked. A man reaps what he sows. Whoever sows to please their flesh, from the flesh will reap destruction; whoever sows to please the Spirit, from the Spirit will reap eternal life. Let us not become weary in doing good, for at the proper time we will reap a harvest if we do not give up. Therefore, as we have opportunity, let us do good to all people, especially to those who belong to the family of believers.

Whatever other people sow into their lives is what they will reap.

Whatever they tried to sow into your life is not what you will reap unless you decide to take the bad seeds and plant them into your own heart and mind.

I had to repeat that to myself over and over.

If we don't want to reap a future filled with relational distrust, bitter perspectives, slander that feels justified, and black clouds of negativity, then we must make the choice not to plant the seeds of unresolved hurt.

I want so much more for my life. And I want so much more for your life as well. We weren't made to just sow and reap constant pain. I love how Psalm 24:3–4 reminds us we were made to ascend upward: "Who may ascend the mountain of the LORD? Who may stand in his holy place? The one who has clean hands and a pure heart."

When life gets hard, we may feel justified if our hearts also get hard and the lens through which we see the world becomes tainted by past hurts. When this happens, we stop believing the best can still happen in our circumstances. We stop believing the best about people. We carry the wrong that one group of people did to us into other relationships and become overly guarded and overly suspicious that history will repeat itself. We can easily start assuming these other people in another organization will hurt us, too, and we start assigning to them wrong intentions they don't have.

But friend, let's make a different choice. Let's sow better so we can reap better. When life gets hard, let your heart stay soft. Let your thoughts stay true. Don't fill in the gaps with worst-case scenarios. Don't assume what others are thinking. You can listen to your discernment. If something feels off or untrue, ask questions, verify answers, and realize sometimes people aren't honest. But at the same time, remember there are many other people who are honest, true, and real.

There are still good-hearted people. People who want the best for you. People who cling to the truth of God's Word and encourage you with the wisdom-filled words from it. Do life with those people. Embrace the gift of those people.

Even though life may look different than you thought it would, it can still be stunningly beautiful. Make the choice right here and right now that you're going to let your heart stay soft and believe there's still goodness and good people and good churches and good organizations and good jobs.

How do I know this to be true?

Because it's true of me, and it's true of you. We aren't perfect . . . but we are people who have made the decision to be purposeful in sowing good and trustworthy and honorable seeds. Now, let's go invest wisely in the next place we land. The goodness we sow will be such a gift to others. But it's also a gift to ourselves, because when we lay our head on the pillow each night, despite what others have done that day, we will have the sweet serenity God gives to those with clean hands and a pure heart.

One More Thing I Want You to Know

Let's dive a little deeper into church hurt. Sometimes what makes hurtful church experiences so painful is not having access to leaders and therefore not having the opportunity to have the conversation in which we get to voice our concerns. Or it's hard to figure out who within the organization is a safe person who will want to listen and be willing to talk things through.

When we can't address what happened, it can feel like resolution is impossible. Yet the intensity of hurt has a driving energy that makes us seek validation for how wrongly things were handled. In an effort to "get it off our chest," we talk about it. Of course we do! But here's where we have to be so careful. Asking to process the pain with a few safe people in our lives is very different from using those conversations to retaliate with harsh words.

Processing is for the purpose of healing what deeply hurt us as we seek to move on in healthy ways. Verbal retaliation is for the purpose of recruiting others to join us in tearing the church down.

I'm not saying we shouldn't use our voices. But I do want us to pause and think about what we are really hoping to accomplish.

Maybe we want fairness and a resolution that makes the wrong things right.

Maybe we want the church leaders to apologize and to learn from this, so our pain doesn't feel so pointless.

Maybe we want that moment where we see the compassion on the leader's face that assures us that, even though this situation went poorly, this person is still good . . . their sermons were legitimate . . . they're willing to do the right thing like we assumed someone in this position should . . . and the years we invested in helping build this ministry weren't a waste.

Honestly, I think we want to know, especially when it comes to people who do God's work, that it isn't all a sham. And it can be really easy to suddenly draw straight lines from some of "God's people" being untrustworthy to the church as a whole being untrustworthy.

But let's say these conversations aren't possible and reconciliation is highly unlikely. What are our options?

We can decide to stay at the church in question and work on making peace with what happened. We can draw healthy boundaries so we don't get hurt the same way again. We can seek to be a light and an example of what it looks like to be so close to Christ that wrong behaviors of others don't knock us off our beam.

Or we can stay and try to be a conduit of change. I have a close friend who has seen her whole church make wise changes with women who feel unsafe in their marriages. From top leadership to lay leaders, they've all been trained in how to help women who are in destructive marriages. And it was all because one woman stayed and advocated for more than twenty years until she saw what she'd been praying for come about.

Another option we have is to decide to leave the church in question and take time to heal, with the intent that this isn't a permanent break from all churches. We can ask our friends to hold us accountable to find a body of believers we can be a part of once again.

Or we can back away from church completely by rationalizing that it's just not worth opening ourselves up once more when we might have our trust broken all over again.

I am not advocating that you stay or leave. I do pray you don't back away from church forever, but I don't want to tell you what to do. I just want to give you a lot to think through and pray about.

Now, play each of those scenarios out. Where does each of these choices lead you? What is the cost to you, and what are the benefits for each of these choices? And most importantly, where is God leading you?

As I think about the sowing and reaping principle, if I want to become more and more like Christ, I can't move further and further away from His church. Jesus knew the struggles we would face, and He gave us the gift of the church to be the support system we would need as we navigate life in this sin-soaked world.

Last week, I stood in church and let the praise songs envelop me. I got so choked up, thinking there is no other place on the planet that sounds more like heaven. I've been hurt by a ministry leader, yes. But not by Jesus. I've been hurt—but not by His design for the way church can be. I've been hurt—but not by all leaders in ministry.

I was glad the praise and worship part of the service lasted longer than normal that Sunday. I honestly didn't want it to end. I breathed in all the goodness and thanked God I hadn't stayed at home.

Bonus Resource

Trust Is a Track Record

10 Scriptural Truths to Remember God's Faithfulness

•

When we are struggling to trust the Lord, we must remind our hearts that God is who He says He is and will do what He says He will do. God's character is always His personal promise to us and something we can consistently count on, no matter how uncertain our circumstances may seem. In fact, He's established a track record of trustworthiness in the pages of Scripture we can turn to in order to trace His presence in our own lives! Here are ten truths to pray through when you're struggling to trust God with circumstances that you have lots of questions about or that don't seem to make any sense.

Read This Truth:

"God is not human, that he should lie,
not a human being, that he should
change his mind.
Does he speak and then not act?
Does he promise and not fulfill?"
(Numbers 23:19)

Pray This Prayer:

Lord,

I confess that so often I equate Your trustworthiness with what I've experienced in my relationships with others. But Your Word reminds me that You are not like humans—You always tell the truth, You are always the same, You always follow through, You always keep Your promises. I want to let these realities sink down deep into my soul and comfort my heart as I wrestle through my doubts that You'll really come through for me. Help me remember that just because people have hurt me, it doesn't mean that You will.

In Jesus' name, amen.

Read This Truth:

"Let us then approach God's throne of grace with confidence, so that we may receive mercy and find grace to help us in our time of need." (Hebrews 4:16)

Pray This Prayer:

Father,

You are good. Thank You for making a way for me to come to You with every need, prayer, hope, and desire. Knowing You openly invite me into Your presence makes me feel safe and accepted even when life's circumstances leave me fearful and alone. I'm so grateful for the gifts of mercy and grace You so freely give to me. You are faithful, and I will always look to You as the source of my help.

In Jesus' name, amen.

Read This Truth:

"Do not be anxious about anything, but in every situation, by prayer and petition, with thanksgiving, present your requests to God. And the peace of God, which transcends all understanding, will guard your hearts and your minds in Christ Jesus." (Philippians 4:6–7)

Pray This Prayer:

Lord,

I'm stopping right now to bring every anxious thought to You. In this moment, I open up my hands to symbolically let go of everything I've been holding on to that You've asked me to release. I'm laying these worries, prayer requests, trust issues, and difficult relationships at Your feet, fully aware that You are in control. I acknowledge that I am powerless to control others. I ask for the supernatural peace only You can provide to protect both my heart and mind, and for Your strength to resist picking these worries back up again.

In Jesus' name, amen.

Read This Truth:

"The LORD is gracious and righteous;
> our God is full of compassion."
(Psalm 116:5)

Pray This Prayer:

Father,

Sometimes my heart is tempted to forget all You've done for me, especially when I'm dealing with a situation that seems like it will never get better. But right now, as a measure of trust, I want to declare these truths out loud: You are gracious. You are righteous. You are full of compassion. Lord, I know You love me and care for me every second of every day. Even when my circumstances and feelings beg me to doubt You, I know You are faithful. Help me live like I believe this, no matter what I face.

In Jesus' name, amen.

Read This Truth:

"I will lead the blind by ways they have not
known,
> along unfamiliar paths I will guide them;

> I will turn the darkness into light before them
> and make the rough places smooth.
> These are the things I will do;
> I will not forsake them." (Isaiah 42:16)

Pray This Prayer:

Lord,

Your Word gives me so much hope. When I read about how You've shown up for Your people throughout history, it helps me see how You show up for me as well. Today, I ask for You to lead me along the unfamiliar roads in front of me. I pray You will render the evil threatening to overtake me powerless by shining Your light onto their sinful schemes and lies. What is brought into the light can no longer run rampant in the dark. And I am trusting You to go before me to work out the details before they overwhelm me. You are a trustworthy God and I will not run ahead of You.

In Jesus' name, amen.

Read This Truth:

> "He reached down from on high and took hold of me;
> he drew me out of deep waters.
> He rescued me from my powerful enemy,
> from my foes, who were too strong for me.
> They confronted me in the day of my disaster,
> but the LORD was my support.
> He brought me out into a spacious place;
> he rescued me because he delighted in
> me." (Psalm 18:16–19)

Pray This Prayer:

God,

I have seen You take hold of me and draw me out of the deep waters in so many situations before. You have come through for me when others have been against me. You have been my ultimate support, always there for me, even when I find my heart straying from You. Thank You, Lord, for being my Rescuer and for caring so intimately for me.

In Jesus' name, amen.

Read This Truth:

"Surely God is my salvation;
   I will trust and not be afraid.
The LORD, the LORD himself, is my strength and
   my defense;
      he has become my salvation." (Isaiah 12:2)

Pray This Prayer:

Father,

I want to borrow the sentiments of Isaiah here and speak Your Word over my hesitations and fears: "God, You are my salvation; I will trust and not be afraid. You are my strength and my defense; You have become my salvation." Yes, Lord, I will absolutely place my full confidence in You. You have proven Yourself trustworthy time and time again, and for that I am grateful.

In Jesus' name, amen.

Read This Truth:

"To humans belong the plans of the heart,
>   but from the LORD comes the proper
>   answer of the tongue.
All a person's ways seem pure to them,
>   but motives are weighed by the LORD.
Commit to the LORD whatever you do,
>   and he will establish your plans."
(Proverbs 16:1–3)

Pray This Prayer:

Lord,

I admit that I have desires for how I want things to turn out and I've made many plans for my life, sometimes without consulting You first. But right now, I want to fully recognize You have the final say; Your plans are so much better than mine. Even when I don't understand what You are doing, I will remain close to You and I will daily declare that I trust You. I will commit everything I do to You and follow Your faithful guidance on the perfect path You've determined, not one I've manufactured on my own.

In Jesus' name, amen.

Read This Truth:

"Jesus Christ is the same yesterday and today and forever."
(Hebrews 13:8)

Pray This Prayer:

Jesus,

It's so difficult to live in a world where things are constantly shifting: jobs, finances, relationships, feelings, family dynamics, politics. It can all be too much sometimes, like I can't count on anything to remain stable. And just because someone seems truthful today doesn't mean they will always be a person of integrity. But I'm learning that I was never meant to rely on anything or anyone in this life for ultimate stability except for You. In the middle of uncertainty, You are certain. In the middle of change, You remain unchanged. You are the same yesterday and today and forever, and that brings me peace.

In Your name, amen.

Read This Truth:

"For the eyes of the LORD range throughout the earth to strengthen those whose hearts are fully committed to him." (2 Chronicles 16:9)

Pray This Prayer:

God,

I want to be found as someone with a heart that is fully committed to You. Though people have broken my trust and life circumstances have broken me down in so many ways, I choose to turn to You for the strength I need today and every day. Only You have the perfect track record of trustworthiness, and I'm learning to not only be okay with that, but to find great comfort in it.

In Jesus' name, amen.

Follow-ups from Lysa

•

Getting the Help You Need

Dear friend,

For some of you this book will be exactly what you needed to help you handle broken trust and navigate your healing when this happens. For some this book might be a guide for repairing trust that's been damaged. But for others this book might help you see that distrust is actually the wisest choice you can make. Because I'm not a licensed counselor and this book doesn't take the place of therapy, please know there are some difficult realities in life that you will want a licensed Christian counselor to help you navigate. Please be honest about your need for counseling help. I am so thankful for the professionals who have lovingly helped lead me through my darkest days. It's always been important to me that the professional counselors I've seen have a deeply committed personal relationship with Jesus and understand the battle must be fought in both the physical and spiritual realm. A great resource to find a Christian counselor in your area is the American Association of Christian Counselors at aacc.net. With counselors in all fifty states, their heart is to connect people who hurt with people who help.

I'm praying for you, dear friend.

Much love,

Some Important Notes to Consider on Abuse

A couple of times throughout this book, I've referenced not excusing away abuse or dysfunctional behavior. You know from reading so much about my personal experiences, my heart is very tender and compassionate toward anyone facing destructive relational realities. I wanted to provide this information, both as a point of compassion and clarity around what abuse is and as a way to potentially find help if you're in an abusive situation.

In an article published by *Psychology Today*, I found this definition of abuse:

> Abuse within families is behaviorally nuanced and emotionally complex. Always, it is within a dynamic of power and control that emotional and physical abuse is perpetuated.
>
> Abuse may manifest as physical (*throwing, shoving, grabbing, blocking pathways, slapping, hitting, scratches, bruises, burns, cuts, wounds, broken bones, fractures, damage to organs, permanent injury, or even murder*), sexual (*suggestive flirtatiousness, propositioning, undesired or inappropriate holding, kissing, fondling of sexual parts, oral sex, or any kind of forceful sexual activity*), or emotional (*neglect, harassment, shaming, threatening, malicious tricks, blackmail, unfair punishments, cruel or degrading tasks, confinement, abandonment*).[19]

So, what does the Bible say about abuse, and what do we do about it? Let's look at what Paul wrote to Timothy:

> But understand this, that in the last days there will come times of difficulty. For people will be lovers of self, lovers of money, proud, arrogant, abusive, disobedient to their parents, ungrateful, unholy, heartless, unappeasable, slanderous, without self-control, brutal, not loving good, treacherous, reckless, swollen with conceit, lovers of

pleasure rather than lovers of God, having the appearance of godliness, but denying its power. Avoid such people. (2 Timothy 3:1–5 ESV)

I'm thankful for verses like these that clearly state to avoid abusive people. But how to avoid them and exactly how this is carried out is so very complex. It's impossible to put a broad, sweeping formula on top of hard relationships. There are so many factors that must be sorted out with people trained to recognize danger and to help lead those in abusive situations to know what to do and how to do it.

Here are some things to consider:

- It is good to have wise people speaking into our lives and to process life concerns with godly mentors and trusted friends. Here's a good verse to help discern people of wisdom in your life:

    Who is wise and understanding among you? By his good conduct let him show his works in the meekness of wisdom. But if you have bitter jealousy and selfish ambition in your hearts, do not boast and be false to the truth. This is not the wisdom that comes down from above, but is earthly, unspiritual, demonic. For where jealousy and selfish ambition exist, there will be disorder and every vile practice. But the wisdom from above is first pure, then peaceable, gentle, open to reason, full of mercy and good fruits, impartial and sincere. And a harvest of righteousness is sown in peace by those who make peace. (James 3:13–18 ESV)

- These trusted friends and godly mentors speaking wisdom into our lives can help us recognize behaviors that cross the line and should be brought to the attention of a professional counselor educated on the issues at hand or, in more urgent situations, to the attention of authorities.

If you need to find a professional Christian counselor in your area, both Focus on the Family and the American Association of Christian Counselors have recommendations listed on their websites, or your church may also have a list of trusted Christian counselors they recommend.

Please know, friend, you are loved, you are not alone, and you don't have to walk through this without help. Remember, the person who is hurting you needs help that only trained professionals can give them. Getting the proper authorities involved isn't being unloving . . . it's actually for your safety and theirs.

Acknowledgments

•

One of the most challenging parts of my healing journey has been to let it unfold. I wanted to speed up my healing. I wanted to know how much longer the hurting would last. I was so tired emotionally, physically, and spiritually. I realized healing would take time. I also realized time doesn't heal all wounds. It's what we plant in the course of time that determines if we heal or not.

There is no formula for this journey. And we can't expect God to do things in our way and in our timing. In that sacred space between the ruins and the glimpses of restoration, I must accept the mystery of God.

And not just accept it but be grateful for it.

I never again want to limit my life down to outcomes of my own design. Instead, I want to live in the anticipation of God's goodness. It's there. We just have to make a point to notice it.

And on the days when I am blinded by my tears, these are my friends who both sit on my bed and cry with me and then grab my hand and say, "Let's go. It won't be like you expected. But it will be good. And some days will be astonishingly breathtaking."

There are so many people whose fingerprints could be found throughout these pages. It would take me another entire book to properly thank everyone . . . the people who have walked beside me, prayed for me, processed this message with me, and even lent their own experiences that made their way into the writing of this book. I am forever grateful for you, your friendship, and for the honor of doing life with you.

To the team who worked alongside me day in and day out on this book, more than helping me get the words right, you helped me get the living of this message right.

I had resistance, you offered assurance.

I had doubts, you offered confidence.

I had so many uncertainties, you offered head nods and enthusiasm that this was the book to write next.

I had dangling participles and wonky verb tenses, you offered editorial wisdom.

I had misspellings and mixed metaphors, you offered smiling emojis with your corrections.

I had theological and therapeutic questions, you offered well-researched answers.

I had unorganized files, you offered the beauty of the Google doc.

I had lulls when I got lost in all my overthinking, you offered conversations and brainstorms and your very best thoughts.

I love you. I love working together, processing life together, being honest about our struggles while studying together, and celebrating our victories together. And I really love that we found our way to this message and worked through this message . . . together.

Chaz: You helped me see that while broken trust is brutal, it can also be the most beautiful part of redemption. I didn't know if I could ever feel safe enough to let my heart be open to a new marriage, a new life. Thank you for your never-ending patience and your always-available embrace. And for helping me remember how fun life can be.

ACKNOWLEDGMENTS

All my kids: You lived this message alongside me. We didn't just survive but we decided to thrive. What a beautiful life that emerged from the darkest ashes. Special shoutout to Hope and Michael who didn't just live this message but who also helped develop the content.

Meredith, Leah, Shae, Amanda, Joel, Jim, Candace, and Mel: Sometimes I don't know where my words end and yours begin. Every paragraph in this book was processed and written alongside you. How can I ever thank you for being the most stellar team and my very best friends? I love you.

Madi, Kaley, Tori, Kelsie, Karen, Anna, Haley, Victoria, Melanie, Morgan, Claire, Stephanie, Jamie, Esther, Nicole, Jasmine, Bethany, Crystal
 Barb, Glynnis
 Jessica, Janene, Andrew, Bria, Dave, Don, MacKenzie, Kristen, John, Emily, Flavia
 And a special thank you to my Early Reader Group who read the earliest version of this manuscript and helped me turn it into a book worth reading.

Notes

1. "Emotional Trauma and the 'Diamond Brain,'" Amen Clinics (blog), October 14, 2021, https://www.amenclinics.com/blog/emotional -trauma-and-the-diamond-brain/.
2. "Emotional Trauma and the 'Diamond Brain.'"
3. You can watch my episode of "Scan My Brain with Dr. Amen" here: "Battling Past Emotional Trauma," YouTube, October 3, 2023, https://www.youtube.com/watch?v=XQqVIUzGGt0.
4. "What Is EMDR Therapy?" EMDR Institute, https://www.emdr.com /what-is-emdr/.
5. Lysa TerKeurst, *Uninvited* (Nashville: Nelson Books, 2016), 215–217.
6. Pamela Li, "Neuroception: The Brain's Subconscious Threat Detector," Parenting for Brain, January 13, 2024, https://www .parentingforbrain.com/neuroception/.
7. Naomi Eisenberger and George Kohlrieser, "Lead with Your Heart, Not Just Your Head," *Harvard Business Review*, November 16, 2012, https://hbr.org/2012/11/are-you-getting-personal-as-a.
8. Eisenberger and Kohlrieser, "Lead with Your Heart"; C. Nathan Dewall, Geoff MacDonald, and Naomi I. Eisenberger, "Acetaminophen Reduces Social Pain: Behavioral and Neural Evidence," *Psychological Science* 21, no. 7 (July 2010): 931–37, https:// doi.org/10.1177/0956797610374741.
9. Hilary Jacobs Hendel, "Ignoring Your Emotions Is Bad for Your Health:

Here's What to Do About It," *Time*, February 27, 2018, https://time
.com/5163576/ignoring-your-emotions-bad-for-your-health/.

10. Please see video 6 of the curriculum (ISBN 9780310145707) for a
more in-depth dive into biblical discernment.

11. Leland Ryken, James C. Wilhoit, Tremper Longman III, eds.,
Dictionary of Biblical Imagery (Downers Grove, IL: InterVarsity Press,
2000), 207.

12. John N. Oswalt, *The Book of Isaiah, Chapters 1–39*, The New
International Commentary on the Old Testament (Grand Rapids:
Eerdmans, 1986), 560.

13. David Guzik, "Hebrews 11—Examples of Faith to Help the
Discouraged," Enduring Word, 2018, https://enduringword.com/bible
-commentary/hebrews-11/.

14. C. H. Spurgeon, "God's Thoughts of Peace, and Our Expected End," in
The Metropolitan Tabernacle Pulpit Sermons, vol. 33 (London: Passmore
& Alabaster, 1887), 303–304. This quote derives from two sections of
the same sermon from Spurgeon that I've presented together.

15. Lysa TerKeurst and Dr. Joel Muddamalle, *30 Days with Jesus:
Experiencing His Presence Throughout the Old and New Testaments*
(Nashville: Thomas Nelson, 2023), 41.

16. "Music and the Vagus Nerve: How Music Affects the Nervous System
and Mental Health," Music Health, https://www.musichealth.ai/blog
/music-and-the-vagus-nerve.

17. Nicki Koziarz (@nickikoziarz), expired Instagram post.

18. Simone Marie, "Can You Get 'Stuck' at the Age You Experienced
Trauma?" PsychCentral, last updated January 5, 2022, https://
psychcentral.com/ptsd/signs-trauma-has-you-stuck.

19. Blake Griffin Edwards, "Secret Dynamics of Emotional, Sexual, and
Physical Abuse," *Psychology Today*, February 23, 2019, https://www
.psychologytoday.com/us/blog/progress-notes/201902/secret-dynamics
-emotional-sexual-and-physical-abuse.

About the Author

•

Photo by Kelsie McGarty

Lysa TerKeurst Adams is president and chief visionary officer of Proverbs 31 Ministries and the author of seven *New York Times* bestsellers, including *Good Boundaries and Goodbyes, Forgiving What You Can't Forget,* and *It's Not Supposed to Be This Way.* She enjoys life with her husband, Chaz, and her kids and grandkids. Connect with her at www.LysaTerKeurst.com or on social media @LysaTerKeurst.

About Proverbs 31 Ministries

Lysa TerKeurst Adams is president and chief visionary officer of Proverbs 31 Ministries.

If you were inspired by *I Want to Trust You, but I Don't* and desire to deepen your own personal relationship with Jesus Christ, we have just what you're looking for.

Proverbs 31 Ministries exists to be a trusted friend who will take you by the hand and walk by your side, leading you one step closer to the heart of God through:

Free *First* 5 Bible study app
Free online daily devotions
Circle 31 Book Club
The Proverbs 31 Ministries Podcast
Therapy and Theology Podcast
COMPEL Pro Writers Training
She Speaks Conference
Books and resources

Our desire is to help you to know the Truth and live the Truth. Because when you do, it changes everything.

For more information about Proverbs 31 Ministries, visit
www.Proverbs31.org

An Invitation from Lysa

Photo by Meshali Mitchell

When my family and I were trying to recover from the darkest season of our lives, I prayed one day we would be able to use our experiences to help others find healing. I dreamed of inviting friends like you to my home.

With this vision we built Haven Place, and in recent years hundreds of women have attended our counseling intensives. These are unique retreats with some of the best Christian therapists who specialize in helping women heal from emotional and relational trauma. You'll also have time with Dr. Joel Muddamalle, learning what the Bible says about hard relational topics.

Plus, I'll be there teaching sessions and meeting with you in my living room when we break out into small groups. We limit these intensives to only fifty women with no more than ten to twelve in each small group. These three days will give you the emotional fortitude and biblical confidence to take the next steps toward moving forward in healthy ways.

Healing and hope have become the anthem songs, prayers, and shouts of victory rising from this place that will be a true sanctuary for your heart and soul.

If you'd like more information, visit www.HavenPlace.org.

3 STEPS TO RELEASE SKEPTICISM AND TRY TRUSTING AGAIN

BY LYSA TERKEURST

....

When you're still dealing with the emotional fallout of broken trust, all relational risk can feel like too much relational risk. But what if we're potentially missing out on new relationships that could bring us great joy, all because we're so focused on not getting hurt again?

Learn to address your hesitations and make progress toward trusting the right people with this additional resource from Lysa.

Download this resource for FREE today at
proverbs31.org/trustagain

Companion Bible Study
for Your Church or Small Group

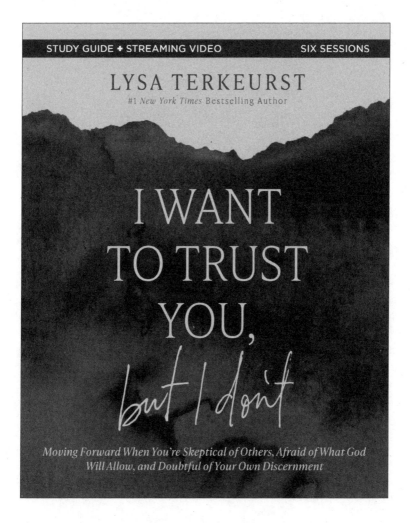

STUDY GUIDE + STREAMING VIDEO   SIX SESSIONS

LYSA TERKEURST
#1 *New York Times* Bestselling Author

I WANT
TO TRUST
YOU,
but I don't

Moving Forward When You're Skeptical of Others, Afraid of What God Will Allow, and Doubtful of Your Own Discernment

AVAILABLE NOW
and streaming online at StudyGateway.com

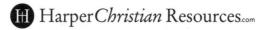

What should I read next?

These two books from Lysa go hand-in-hand with what you're learning in *I Want to Trust You, but I Don't*

 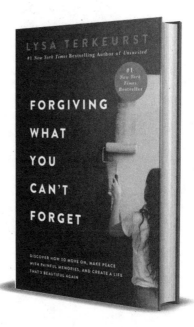

Available wherever books and audiobooks are sold

LYSA TERKEURST